I0081304

TASC®

STRATEGY

WINNING MULTIPLE CHOICE STRATEGIES FOR THE TEST ASSESSING SECONDARY COMPLETION®

COMPLETE
TEST PREPARATION INC.
WWW.TEST-PREPARATION.CA

ISBN-13: 978-1928077268 (Complete Test Preparation Inc.)
ISBN-10: 1928077269

Version 9 Updated July 2025

Published by
Complete Test Preparation Inc.
Victoria BC Canada

Visit us on the web at https://www.test-preparation.ca
Printed in the USA

About Complete Test Preparation Inc.

Why Us?
The Complete Test Preparation Team has been publishing high quality study materials since 2005, with a catalog of over 145 titles, in English, French and Chinese, as well as ESL curriculum for all levels.

To keep up with the industry changes we update everything all the time!

And the best part?
With every purchase, you're helping people all over the world improve themselves and their education. So thank you in advance for supporting this mission with us! Together, we are truly making a difference in the lives of those often forgotten by the system.

Charities that we support -
https://www.test-preparation.ca/charities-and-non-profits/

You have definitely come to the right place.
If you want to spend your valuable study time where it will help you the most - we've got you covered today and tomorrow.

Feedback

We welcome your feedback. Email us at feedback@test-preparation.ca with your comments and suggestions. We carefully review all suggestions and often incorporate reader suggestions into upcoming versions. As a Print on Demand Publisher, we update our products frequently.

Contents

GETTING STARTED

CONGRATULATIONS! By deciding to take the TASC®, you have taken the first step toward a great future! Of course, there is no point in taking this important examination unless you intend to do your best to earn the highest grade you possibly can. That means getting yourself organized and discovering the best approaches, methods and strategies to master the material. Yes, that will require real effort and dedication on your part, but if you are willing to focus your energy and devote the study time necessary, before you know it you will be finished the exam with a great mark!

We know that taking on a new endeavour can be a scary, and it is easy to feel unsure of where to begin. That's where we come in. This study guide is designed to help you improve your test-taking skills, show you a few tricks and increase both your competency and confidence.

The Test Assessing Secondary Completion®

The TASC® exam is composed of five sections, Reading, Writing, Mathematics, Science, and Social Studies. It measures examinees' levels of achievement and readiness for college and the workforce as outlined by the Common Core State Standards.

Test Strategy

This is a book about improving your score by using proven test strategies. This is different from other books such as a study guide, or a practice test. Even though we do provide lots of information to study and practice test questions, this book is about how to tackle multiple choice questions.

A Better Score Is Possible

Worried about that big exam coming up? Do you think you're just not a good test-taker, especially when it comes to standardized tests? The good news is that you're not alone. The bad news is that millions of people are left behind through objective testing, simply because they're not good test-takers - even though they may know the material. They don't know how to handle the format well or understand what's expected of them.
This is especially true of the multiple-choice test. Test-takers are given a lot of support for taking essay-style tests. They're helped with skills such as grammar and spelling. However, little is offered for the multiple-choice exam. This is although thousands of people find multiple-choice to be the most challenging kind of test. Here are some reasons that so many people have difficulties with multiple-choice:

The Broad Range. Because the questions are so short, a lot of ground is covered in the test. Who's to know what to study with so much material covered?

Time Limits. Most standardized tests have time limits, which adds an extra layer of pressure.

Trickery. Many test-designers think that it is too easy to guess a multiple-choice question correctly, so they intentionally make the questions tricky.

Bluffing Not Allowed. With an essay test, you can try to bluff your way through it. Not so with multiple-choice. The answer is either right or wrong.

Difficult to Write. It's not easy for a test-writer to design a good multiple-choice test. Sometimes, they make them overly difficult.

Shuffled Content. Multiple-choice tests tend to throw the questions in at random, in no particular order. You could be answering a question about the 1700s and then about the 2004 Presidential election.

These challenges mean that you have to be familiar with a wider range of material than on other kinds of exams. You'll need to know specific vocabulary, rules, names, dates, etc.

There are, however, a few advantages to you, the test-taker, with a multiple-choice test. For instance, because there are more multiple-choice items on a test than other types, each question tends to have a lower point value. You can afford to miss a few and still be okay. Also, if you're writing a fill-in-the blank or essay test, you have to rely totally on memory for the answer. With a multiple-choice exam, you know that the correct answer is somewhere in the question. You just have to decide which one it is. Often, seeing the right answer will trigger your memory, and you'll recognize it instantly.

Keep in mind, though, the test-writer knows that one advantage of multiple-choice is the fact the answer is on the page. Therefore, many test-writers include what is called a "distracter." This is a possible answer that is designed to look like the correct answer, but which is actually wrong. We'll talk about this again later, but an example would be the question: "Who is known for posting 95 theses on a church wall?" Among the answers might be Martin Luther and Martin Luther King. Because the student vaguely remembers the name "Martin Luther" from the course materials, there's a chance that he'll select the incorrect "Martin Luther King."

Who Does Well On Multiple-Choice Exams?

With so many challenges working against you on the multiple-choice exam, what's the answer? Is there a way to improve your chances and your score? There is! The point of this book is not to discourage you, but to make you aware that there are strategies and tips that you can incorporate to raise your test score. Before we get into the specific strategies, let's take a general look at who does best on these types of tests.

Those who know the material. This should go without saying, but the thing that will most raise your test score will be if you know the material that's going to be covered. While the strategies we'll discuss later will help you even with questions you're unsure of, the best thing you can do is learn the rules, dates, names, and concepts that you'll be tested on.

Those who have a calm, cool demeanor when taking a test. Panicking can cause you to forget the information you think you know. Confidence goes a long way toward a better mark on multiple-choice.

Those who meditate or pray before the test. Don't laugh. It's a fact that people who meditate or pray, depending on their beliefs, enter a test room more confidently, and do better on the exam.

Those who operate on logic rather than instinct. Those who take a multiple-choice test based on instinct will be tempted to overlook the stated facts, and let emotion rule.

Those who have a system. Most of the book will deal with this, but you should not just guess randomly on questions you don't know. You must have a systematic strategy.

Answering Multiple-Choice Step-by-Step

HERE IS A TEST QUESTION:

Which of the following is a helpful tip for taking a multiple-choice test?

a. Answering "B" for all questions.

b. Eliminate all answers that you know cannot be true.

c. Eliminate all answers that seem like they might be true.

d. Cheat off your neighbor.

If you answered B, you are correct. Even if you are not positive about the answer, try to eliminate of as many choices as possible. Think of it this way: If every item on your test has four possible answers, and if you guess on one of those four answers, you have a one-in-four chance (25%) of getting it right. This means you should get one question right for every four that you guess.

However, if you can get rid of two answers, then your chances improve to one-in-two chances, or 50%. That means you will get a correct answer to every two that you guess.

So much for an obvious tip for improving your multiple-choice score. There are many other tips that you may or may not have considered, which will give your grade a boost. Remember, though, that none of these tips are infallible. In fact, many test-writers know these tips and deliberately write questions that will confound your system. Usually, however, you will do better on the test if you put these tips into practice.

By familiarizing yourself with these tips, you increase your chances and who knows; you might just get a lucky break and increase your score by a few points!

Answering Step-by-Step

It might seem complicated and unnecessary to follow a formula for answering a multiple-choice question. After you have practiced this formula for a while, though, it will come naturally and will not take any time at all. Try to follow these steps below on each question.

Step 1. Cover up the answers while you read the question. See the material in your mind's eye and try to envision what the correct answer is before you expose the answers on the answer sheet.

Step 2. Uncover the responses.

Step 3. Eliminate or Estimate. Cross out every choice that you know is ridiculous, absurd or clearly wrong. Then work with the answers that remain.

Step 4. Watch for distracters. A distracter is an answer that looks very similar to the correct answer, but is put there to trip you up. If you see two answers that are strikingly similar, the chances are good that one of them is correct. For instance, if you are asked the term for the distance around a square, and two of the responses are "periwinkle" and "perimeter," you can guess that one of these is probably correct, since the words look similar (both start with "peri-"). Guess one of these two and your chances of correcting selecting "perimeter" are 50/50. More on this below.

Step 5. Check! If you see the answer that you saw in your mind, put a light check mark by it and then see if any of the other choices are better. If not, mark that response as your answer.

Step 6. If all else fails, guess. If you cannot envision the correct response in your head, or figure it out by reading the passage, and if you are left totally clueless as to what the answer should be, guess.

The TASC does not penalize for wrong answers so guessing is a good strategy if all else fails!

There is a common myth that says choice “C” has a statistically greater chance of being correct. This may be true if your professor is making the test, however, most standardized tests computer generated today and the choices are randomized. We do not recommend choosing “C” for every questions as a strategy.

That is a quick introduction to multiple-choice to get us warmed up. Next we move onto the strategies and practice test questions section. Each multiple-choice strategy is explained, followed by practice questions using the strategy. Opposite this page is a bubble sheet for answering.

Answer Sheet

	A	B	C	D	E		A	B	C	D	E
1	○	○	○	○	○	26	○	○	○	○	○
2	○	○	○	○	○	27	○	○	○	○	○
3	○	○	○	○	○	28	○	○	○	○	○
4	○	○	○	○	○	29	○	○	○	○	○
5	○	○	○	○	○	30	○	○	○	○	○
6	○	○	○	○	○	31	○	○	○	○	○
7	○	○	○	○	○	32	○	○	○	○	○
8	○	○	○	○	○	33	○	○	○	○	○
9	○	○	○	○	○	34	○	○	○	○	○
10	○	○	○	○	○	35	○	○	○	○	○
11	○	○	○	○	○	36	○	○	○	○	○
12	○	○	○	○	○	37	○	○	○	○	○
13	○	○	○	○	○	38	○	○	○	○	○
14	○	○	○	○	○	39	○	○	○	○	○
15	○	○	○	○	○	40	○	○	○	○	○
16	○	○	○	○	○	41	○	○	○	○	○
17	○	○	○	○	○	42	○	○	○	○	○
18	○	○	○	○	○	43	○	○	○	○	○
19	○	○	○	○	○	44	○	○	○	○	○
20	○	○	○	○	○	45	○	○	○	○	○
21	○	○	○	○	○						
22	○	○	○	○	○						
23	○	○	○	○	○						
24	○	○	○	○	○						
25	○	○	○	○	○						

Strategy Practice Questions

THE FOLLOWING ARE DETAILED STRATEGIES FOR ANSWERING MULTIPLE-CHOICE QUESTIONS WITH PRACTICE QUESTIONS FOR EACH STRATEGY.

Answers appear following this section with a detailed explanation and discussion on each strategy and question, plus tips and analysis.

Strategy 1 - Locate Keywords

For every question, figure out exactly what the question is asking by locating key words that are in the question. Underline the keywords to clarify your thoughts and keep on track.

Directions: Read the passage below, and answer the questions using this strategy.

Free-range is a method of farming where domesticated animals roam freely, or relatively freely, rather than being kept in a pen or cage. Free-range can mean two different things depending on who you talk to. One definition, when talking to a farmer, is a technical description of a farming method. You may have seen free-range or free-run eggs in the supermarket. This is a consumer oriented definition. There are numerous benefits to farmers who practice free-range farming. Certification as a free-range producer allows farmers to charge higher prices and also reduce feed costs. That's not all - free-range methods also improve the general health of animals, which produces a higher-quality product. In addition, free-range farming allows multiple crops on the same land - another significant savings for farmers. Free-range certification is different from organic certification.

1. The free-range method of farming

a. Uses a minimum amount of fencing to give animals more room.

b. Can refer to two different things.

c. Is always a very humane method.

d. Only allows for one crop at a time.

2. Free-range farming is practiced

a. To obtain free-range certification.

b. To lower the cost of feeding animals.

c. To produce higher quality product.

d. All of the above.

3. Free-range farming:

a. Can mean either farmer described or consumer described methods.

b. Is becoming much more popular in many areas.

c. Has many limits and causes prices to go down.

d. Is only done to make the animals happier and healthier.

4. Free-range certification is most important to farmers because:

a. Free-range livestock are less expensive to feed.

b. The price of the product is higher.

c. Both a and b

d. The animals are kept in smaller enclosures, so more can be produced.

Strategy 2 - Watch Negatives

For every question, no matter what type, look for negatives. These can include never, not, and others that will completely change what is being asked.

Directions: Read the passage below, and answer the questions using this strategy.

Grizzly bears exhibit a common feature in nature, sexual dimorphism. This is where there are distinct difference in size or appearance between the sexes of an animal. Male grizzly bears, for example, generally weigh between 400 and 750 pounds, but can weight over 1,000 pounds. Females grizzlies are smaller, weighing 250 – 350 pounds, which is about 38% smaller. Female grizzlies stand about 3 feet at the shoulder, on all fours, and over 6 feet when standing upright. Males are bigger, generally standing 8 feet or more on their hind legs. Grizzlies in different geographical areas also show significant differences. For example, grizzlies from the Yukon River area in Northern Canada are 20% smaller.

5. Sexual dimorphism does not mean

a. Male grizzly bears are the same size as the female of the species.

b. All grizzly bears look the same and are the same size.

c. Grizzly bears can be quite large, and weigh more than half a ton.

d. All of the above

6. The size of a full-grown grizzly bear is never

a. More than 500 pounds.

b. Depends on the bear's sex.

c. Determined simply by diet.

d. Less than 8 feet tall.

7. Grizzly bears from the area of the Yukon River do not

a. Get as big as most other grizzly bears do
b. Get the rich and varied food supply needed
c. Need the same nutrients as other grizzly bears
d. Get less than 7 feet tall, and weigh close to half of a ton

Strategy 3 - Read the Stem Completely

For every question, no matter what type, read the information in the stem and then try to determine the correct answer before you look at the different answers.

Directions: Read the passage below, and answer the questions using this strategy.

Brown bears and grizzly bears are generally considered separate species, although technically, both are classified as Ursus Arctos. Brown bears live in coastal areas of North America where salmon is the primary food source. Bears found inland and in northern habitats are called 'grizzlies.' A sub species of Brown bears found on Kodiak Island, Alaska, have different shaped skulls due to the remote region and independent development.

Black bear, which are smaller and more common, are also a sub species, Ursus Americanus. Black bears are found throughout North America.

8. Grizzly bears, brown bears, and Kodiak bears are all

a. Arctas Ursinas
b. Ursus Arctos
c. Arctos Ursina
d. Ursula Arctic

9. Kodiak brown bears are classified as a different subspecies because

a. They are much larger than other brown bears

b. Their diet is radically different from that of other brown bears

c. They are not true brown bears but instead a mixture of bear species

d. Of their genetics and head shape, as well as their physical isolation

10. The term grizzlies, when referring to the brown bear, is used mainly

a. In eastern areas where the bear grows large

b. Only in snowy areas where there are low year round temperatures

c. In the northern and inland areas

d. In areas where the bear has a silver appearance

11. The term brown bear is normally used

a. When one of the main food sources is salmon

b. When the bear is small

c. When the bear is found inland

d. When the bear has a light brown coat and is very large

Strategy 4 - Consider all the Choices Before Deciding

For every question, no matter what type, make sure to read every option before making your choicc.

Directions: Read the passage below, and answer the questions using this strategy.

Polar bears and grizzlies are different species although there are rare cases of hybrids. Scientists have known the two species are compatible for some time and there are several cases of hybrids in zoos.

In 2006, in Canada's Northwest Territories, a hunter shot what he thought was a polar bear. This bear, however, was slightly different. Like most polar bears, its fur was thick and white, as one would expect of a polar bear. However the bear also had some characteristics of grizzlies, such as long claws, a humped back, and brown patches around its nose, eyes and back.

This odd combination of features from both species soon attracted attention of the Wildlife Genetics International in British Columbia, Canada, which confirmed that this animal was a polar bear grizzly hybrid through DNA testing, and, the first hybrid found in the wild.

This bear appears to be the product of a polar bear mother and a grizzly bear father. Until 2006, there had been no documented cases of a grizzly polar bear hybrid found in the wild.

12. Which grizzly bear features did the hybrid bear have?

a. Brown patches in certain areas
b. Long claws
c. A shallow face
d. All of the above

13. The hybrid bear was the result of

a. A male brown bear and a female grizzly.
b. A female brown bear and a male grizzly bear.
c. A female polar bear and a male grizzly bear.
d. A male polar bear and a female grizzly.

14. The hybrid bear tested in this case was

a. The first known case two different bear species mated successfully.

b. Genetically flawed and prone to many diseases and conditions.

c. A fluke, and a mistake of nature which has never happened.

d. The first proof of a wild bear hybrid species outside of zoos.

15. Modern science

a. Has proven that the cubs from two different species will not survive in almost every case.

b. Has known for some time that these hybrid bears were possible.

c. Completely understands how bear hybrids occur and why this happens in nature.

d. Has studied hundreds of bear hybrids in an attempt to learn more.

Strategy 5 - Elimination

For every question, no matter what type, eliminating obviously incorrect answers narrows the possible choices. Elimination is probably the most powerful strategy for answering multiple-choice.

Directions: Read the passage below, and answer the questions using this strategy.

Peacocks have been admired throughout history for their beautiful plumage and train of the male peafowl, or peacock, with its characteristic eye pattern.

In Greek mythology, Hera, wife of Zuess, and queen of the Gods, placed the hundred eyes of the slain giant Argus on the tail of the peacock, her favorite bird.

The peacock's tail or train, is not actually the tail, but the elongated feathers of the upper tail. These beautiful green-bronze feathers, with the eye pattern, can be seen when the train is fanned out. The actual tail feathers of the peacock are short and grey-colored and can be seen from behind when the train is fanned in a courtship display.

The grey tail feathers can also be seen during molting season, when males drop the feathers in their train. The female peacock is duller compared to the spectacular male. The female is brown, with some green iridescence feathers on her neck.

16. The long colorful tail feathers of the peacock

a. Are only present in the male of the species
b. Are used by both sexes to warn off predators
c. Are normally red and blue
d. Are only present for a very short time each year

17. The differences between the male and female peacock are

a. Size and weight
b. Coloring and tail feather length
c. The female does not ever leave the nest
d. The male sits on and hatches the eggs

18. The term peacock actually refers to

a. Both sexes from the pheasant family
b. The eyes on the tail feathers of the bird
c. The male bird of the peafowl species
d. The female bird of the peafowl species

19. The gray tail feathers on the male peacock can be seen

a. When the bird is startled

b. Only when the bird is searching for food

c. When the peacock lowers the tail feathers to the ground

d. During molting

Strategy 6 - Opposites

For every question, no matter what type, look at answers that are opposites. When two answers are opposites, the odds increase that one of them is the correct answer.

Directions: Read the passage below, and answer the questions using this strategy.

Smallpox is a highly infectious disease unique to humans, caused by two virus, Variola Major and Minor. The Latin name for smallpox is Variola or Variola Vera, which means spotted.

In 1980, the World Health Organization certified that Smallpox had been eradicated. Smallpox is sometimes confused with Chicken Pox, however, they are different virus.

The smallpox virus lives in the small blood vessels in the mouth, throat and skin. This gives a distinct rash in these areas, which turn into blisters. After being exposed to the Smallpox virus, symptoms do not appear for 12 to 17 days.

Variola Major is much more serious virus, with a mortality rate of 30 – 35%. Variola Minor is milder, with a mortality rate of only 1%. Variola Minor has a number of common names, including, alastrim, cottonpox, milkpox, whitepox, and Cuban itch.

Variola Major causes several long-term complications such as scars, commonly on the face, which occurs in about 65 – 85% of the survivors. Other complications, including blindness and deformities from arthritis and other complications are much less common, about 2 – 5%.

20. Smallpox

a. Effects all mammals, including humans

b. Is caused by a bacteria from contact with dead flesh

c. Was called the great pox during the fifteenth century

d. Only affects humans, although other species can carry and transmit the virus

21. Smallpox caused by Variola major has a

a. Thirty to thirty five percent survival rate

b. Sixty percent mortality rate

c. Thirty to thirty five percent mortality rate

d. Sixty percent survival rate

22. Smallpox caused by Variola minor is

a. Much more severe, with more pox and scarring

b. Much less severe, with fewer pox and less scarring

c. Characterized as minor because there are no pox

d. So minor that no treatment or medical attention is needed

23. Smallpox can be fatal

a. In between thirty and thirty five percent of those who catch the virus, depending on the type

b. In between thirty and sixty five percent of those who catch the virus, depending on the type

c. When no medical treatment is available

d. Only in developing countries where medical care is poor

Strategy 7 - Look for Differences

For every question, no matter what type, look at the two choices that seem to be correct and then examine the differences between the two. Refer to the stem to determine the best answer.

Directions: Read the passage below, and answer the questions using this strategy.

Lightning is one of the most amazing natural phenomenon. A popular belief is that lightning cannot strike twice in the same place. This however, is not true - lightning does strike in the same place frequently.

Lightning is an electrical discharge between clouds and the ground, or between two clouds. It is often accompanied with thunder during thunderstorms, dust storms and volcanic eruptions. Every year, there are an estimated 16 million lightning storms worldwide.

Bolts of lightning travel at speeds of 130,000 miles per hour and contain a billion volts of electricity. Lightning bolts can reach temperatures of 54,000° F. This is hot enough to turn sand, some soils or even rock into hollow glass channels, called fulgurites. Fulgurites extend far below the surface.

Lightning is such a common feature of the natural world, there is even a classification for the fear of lightning and thunder, called astraphobia.

Clouds of volcanic ash, as well as dust storms and forest fires can generate enough static electricity to produce lightning.

Scientists do not understand the process of lightning formation, and this is a matter for debate. Scientists have studied causes of lightning, such as wind, humidity, friction, atmospheric pressure, solar winds and accumulation of charged solar particles. Many scientists believe that ice inside clouds is important in causing lightning.

24. Astraphobia is

a. Fear of thunder
b. Fear of thunder and lightning
c. Fear of lightning
d. None of the above

25. Lightning occurs

a. Only in thunderstorms
b. In thunderstorms and dust storms
c. In thunderstorms, volcanic eruptions and dust storms
d. In the upper atmosphere

26. Fulgurites are

a. Made of silica
b. Made of glass
c. Made of sand, soil and rock turned into glass
d. Made of silica and glass

Strategy 8 - Context Clues

Looked at the sentences and the context to determine the best option. Sometimes, the answer may be located right in the passage or question.

Directions: Read the passage below, and answer the questions using this strategy.

Venus is one of the four solar terrestrial planets, or rocky bodies that orbit the sun. Planets are defined as a celestial body moving in an elliptical orbit around a star. Venus is about the same size as Earth. Venus' diameter (12,104 km) is only 650 km. less than Earth's, (12,742 km.) and its mass is 81.5% of Earth's. The Venusian atmosphere is a dense mixture of carbon dioxide with some nitrogen.

Venus orbits the sun every 224.7 days, and is the second-closest planet to the Sun.

Venus, as the second brightest star in the sky, after the moon, reaches an apparent magnitude of −4.6, was named after Venus, the goddess of love and beauty by the Romans. The Romans named all the brightest stars after their Gods and Goddesses. Venus is often called the Morning, or Evening Star. Venus reaches its maximum brightness before sunrise and after sunset

Venus is an inferior planet from Earth, meaning that it is closer to the sun: its elongation reaches a maximum of 47.8°.

27. Apparent magnitude is

a. A measure of darkness
b. A measure of brightness
c. The distance from the moon
d. The distance from the earth

28. The elongation of a planet is

a. The angular distance from the sun, as seen from earth.
b. The distance from the sun
c. The distance form the earth
d. None of the above

29. Terrestrial planets are

a. Made of rock
b. Have people on them
c. The earth and no others
d. The same size as Earth

30. How many planets orbit the sun in less than 224.7 days?

a. 1 planet
b. Only Venus
c. 2 planets
d. 3 planets

Strategy 9 - Try Every Option

For definition questions, try out all the options - one option will fit better than the rest. As you go through the options, use Strategy 5 - Elimination, to eliminate obviously incorrect choices as you go.

Directions: Read the passage below, and answer the questions using this strategy.

Some of the common weather patterns on Earth are rain, wind, fog, and snow. Other weather patterns, generally classified as natural disasters, are hurricanes, tornadoes, typhoons and ice storms. Weather generally happens in the lower portion of the atmosphere, called the troposphere. Some weather can occur in the upper atmosphere, or stratosphere, where it can effect weather in the lower troposphere.

The principle cause of weather is different temperature, barometric pressure and moisture densities in the atmosphere. Weather phenomena in the atmosphere such as the jet stream is caused by the temperature differences in the tropical and polar air, which causes air to move from one to the other. The jet stream generally flows in a Western direction, and there are two or three jet streams in the Northern and Southern Hemispheres at any time.

Instabilities in the flow of the jet stream cause weather systems such as extra-tropical cyclones. Different processes cause weather systems such as monsoons or thunderstorms. Monsoons are caused by a difference in temperature over land and over sea.

Due to the tilt of the Earth's axis, sunlight reaches the

Earth at different angles at different times of the year, creating seasons. In January, the Northern Hemisphere is tilted away from the sun, so sunlight is more direct than in July.

31. The troposphere is

a. The atmosphere's highest strata
b. The atmosphere's lowest strata
c. The atmosphere's middle strata
d. Not part of the atmosphere

32. Monsoons are

a. Caused by instabilities in the jet stream
b. Caused by processes other than instabilities in the jet stream
c. Part of the jet stream
d. Cause the jet stream

33. Extra-tropical cyclones occur

a. In the tropics
b. In temperate zones
c. In the gulf stream
d. In mid-latitudes

34. Tilted means:

a. Slanted
b. Rotating
c. Connected to
d. Bent

Strategy 10 - Work for it

For questions about supporting details, work is the key. Review the passage to locate the right option. Never forget the choices that you are given are designed to confuse, and they may *seem* reasonable answers. However, if they are not mentioned in the text, they are "red herring" answers.

The best answer is the exact answer mentioned in the text.

Directions: Read the passage below, and answer the questions using this strategy.

Ebola is a common term for a group of viruses in the genus Ebola (EBOV), family Filoviridae. There are several species within the Ebola virus genus, with specific strains. Ebola is also a general term for the disease the viruses cause, Ebola hemorrhagic fever. The Ebola virus is transmitted through bodily fluids.

The Ebola virus interferes with the cell and patients die of hypovolemic shock.

The Ebola viruses are similar to the Marburg virus, also in the family Filoviridae. Most viruses are spherical, however, the Ebola viruses have long filaments. The Ebola and Marburg viruses have similar symptoms.

The first outbreak of Ebola occurred near the Ebola River, in the Democratic Republic of the Congo, which the disease and viruses are named after. Ebola is a very serious illness, very contagious and often fatal. The 2014 West African Ebola viral epidemic was the most widespread in history.

The Zaire virus was the first discovered in 1976 and is the most lethal. Ebola first emerged in 1976 in Zaire. An outbreak in Reston, Virginia brought the virus to international attention.

35. The Ebola virus received this name because of

a. The doctor who first discovered the virus
b. The cure that is used to treat those infected
c. The river where the disease was first encountered
d. What the virus does to the body

36. Viruses in the Ebola genus are recognizable

a. Because of their hooked shape
b. Because of their long filaments
c. Due to their oblong heads
d. Because of their unique color

37. One of the most common causes of death from the Ebola family of viruses is

a. Hypovolemic shock due to blood vessel damage
b. Bleeding of the brain that cannot be stopped
c. A heart attack from blood loss and lack of fluids
d. A high fever that cannot be lowered

38. The most deadly strain of the Ebola virus family is the

a. The Reston strain
b. The Ivory Coast strain
c. The Zaire strain
d. The Sudan strain

Strategy 11 - Look at the Big Picture

Details can be tricky when dealing with main idea and summary questions, but do not let the details distract you. Look at the big picture instead of the smaller parts to determine the right answer.

Directions: Read the passage below, and answer the questions using this strategy.

In 2005 researchers found three species of fruit bat carrying the Ebola virus, but not showing disease symptoms. These three species are called natural host, or reservoir species. Scientists have studied plants, insects and birds as potential reservoir species without success. Bats are the only reservoir species scientists have found. Apparently, bats are reservoir species for several viruses.

The first outbreaks, in 1976 and 1979, were in cotton factories where bats lived. Bats were also present in the Marburg infections in 1975 and 1980.

39. The species most suspected as a potential Ebola virus reservoir is

a. Birds
b. Insects
c. Plants
d. Bats

40. Most plant and animal species

a. Can carry the Ebola virus but not become infected
b. Can not carry and transmit the Ebola virus
c. Are responsible for new cases of Ebola viruses
d. Can be infected with one of the Ebola viruses

41. Bats are known for

a. Being carriers of many different viruses, including Ebola

b. Transmitting the Ebola virus through a scratch

c. Being susceptible to the virus and becoming infected

d. Transmitting the Ebola virus through infected droppings

Strategy 12 - Best Possible Answer

Try to determine the best possible answer according to the information given in the passage. Do not be distracted by answers that seem correct or are mostly correct.

Directions: Read the passage below, and answer the questions using this strategy.

Ebola may not be contagious initially but as the disease progresses, bodily fluids are extremely contagious.

Lack of proper equipment and proper hygiene has caused epidemics in poor and isolated areas. Unfortunately, infectious reservoirs generally exist in areas do not have modern hospitals or educated medical staff, adding to the chance of epidemics.

42. Ebola is highly contagious

a. Only when blood is present

b. Only in the first stages before hemorrhaging occurs

c. At all stages of the illness from incubation to recovery

d. Only in the later stages

43. Exposure to the Ebola virus means

a. A death sentence for most patients

b. Isolation for the patient, and proper precautions for all medical personnel to contain the virus

c. The virus will spread rapidly and there is no treatment available

d. A full recovery usually, with very few symptoms

44. Ebola outbreaks commonly occur

a. Because sterilization and containment procedures are not followed or available

b. Due to infected animals in the area

c. Because of rat droppings in homes

d. Because of a contaminated water supply

45. Ebola is

a. More common in advanced nations where treatment makes the disease minor

b. More common in third world and developing countries

c. Fatal in more than ninety-five percent of the cases

d. Highly contagious during the incubation period

Answer Key

Strategy 1 - Keywords in the Question Tell What the Question is Asking

1. B
The question asks about the free range *method* of farming. Here method refers to *type* of farming. "Method" here is the keyword and can be marked or underlined.

2. D
The Question is, "Free-range farming is *practiced* ..." The keyword here is "practiced." Looking at the choices, which all start with "to," it is clear the answer will be about *why* free range ... Also notice that one choice is "All of the above," which here, is the correct answer. However, when "All of the above" is an option, this is a potential Elimination Strategy. All you have to do is find one choice that is incorrect and you can use Strategy 5 - Elimination to eliminate two choices and increase your odds from one in four, to one in two.

3. A
The question is, "Free range farming husbandry ..." From the question, and the *lack* of keywords, together with the choices presented, the answer will be a definition free range farming husbandry.

4. C
The question is, "Free-range certification is *most important* to farmers because ... "The keywords here are "most important." Circle the keywords to keep them clear in your mind. Be careful to choose the best possible answer.

Strategy 2 - Watch Negatives

These four questions all have negatives: does not mean, is never, do not, and is not. These questions exclude possibilities, so if you see any choices that are true, you can eliminate them right away.

5. D

The question asks what sexual dimorphism does *not* mean. Circle the word "not" and keep it firmly in mind. Next, what is sexual dimorphism. Reading the text quickly, sexual dimorphism is related to the female bears being smaller than the males. Probably there are other aspects, but this general definition is all that is needed to answer the question.

First, notice that "All of the above" is choice D. In addition, the question is a negative. So, for choice D to be correct, choices A, B and C must be *in*correct. This narrows down your options. If any of choices A, B or C are correct, then you can eliminate that choice as well as choice D.

Either all the choices are *in*correct, in which case, choice D, "All of the above" is correct.

Choice A, male and females are the same size is incorrect.
Choice B, all grizzly bears look the same and are the same size, is incorrect. Choice C, grizzly bears (plural so *all* grizzly bears) can be large and weigh more than half a ton. This is incorrect since while all grizzly bears are large, female bears weight less than half a ton.

All three choices are incorrect so choice D is the correct answer, "All of the Above," are incorrect.

6. A

First, circle or underline never to show this is a negative question. Now look at the options to find an option that is not true.

Choice A is true as male bears are 1,000 pounds. Place a mark beside this one. It may be tempting to select this option as your answer, but it is important to look at all choices before making a final decision.

Choice B is not true - size does not depend on the sex.
Choice C is not true - size does not depend on diet.
Choice D is not true - males often stand 8 feet.

So choice A is correct.

7. A
First circle "do not" to mark this as a negative question.

Choice A is correct, Yukon River grizzly bears do not get as big as other grizzlies, so put a mark beside it for later consideration. Examine the other choices before making a final decision.

Choice B is not mentioned in the text, and can be eliminated.

Choice C is not mentioned in the text and can be eliminated.

Choice D is true, but this is a negative question so it is false.

Some of the above choices may be true from a common sense point of view, but if they aren't mentioned specifically in the passage, they can be eliminated.

Choice A is correct.

Strategy 3 - Read the Stem Completely

Read the question, and then look for the answer in the text before reading the choices. Reading the choices first will confuse, just as it is meant to do! Do not fall into this trap!

8. B
The choices here are very confusing and are meant to be! Four variations on the latin species name, Ursus Arctos are given, so the question is what version of this latin name is correct, which gives a very straightforward strategy to solving. Since the name is latin, it

is going to stand out in the text. Take the first option, "Arctas Ursinas," and scan the text for something that looks like that. At the end of the second sentence is "Ursus Arctos," which is very close. Next confirm what this sentence refers to, which gives the correct answer, Choice B.

9. D
This question asks why Kodiak brown bears are a different subspecies, and the options are designed to confuse a careless, stressed test-taker. Scan the text for "Kodiak," which appears in the second to last sentence, and answers the question.

10. C
This question asks about the relationship between brown bears and grizzly bears. If you are not careful you will be confused by the choices.

11. A
Read the question, then read the text before trying to answer and avoid confusion.

Strategy 4 - Consider all Choices Before Deciding

In Strategy 3, we learned to find the correct answer in the text before reading the choices. Now you have read the text and have the right answer. The next thing is Strategy 4 - Read *all* the choices. Once you have read all the choices, select the correct choice.

12. D
First, notice that "All of the above" is a choice. So if you find one option that is incorrect, you can eliminate that option and option D, "All of the above." Reading the question first, (Strategy #3) then looking in the text, and then reading all the choices before answering, you can see that choices A, B and C are all correct, so choice D, All of the Above, is the correct choice.
If you had not read all the choices first, then you might be tempted to impulsively choose A, B, or C.

13. C

Looking at the choices, they are designed to confuse with different choices and combinations. Recognizing this, it is therefore important to be extra careful in making your choice. If you are stressed, in a hurry, or not paying attention, you will probably get this question wrong by making an impulsive choice and not reading through all the choices before making a selection.

Referring to the text, you will find the sentence, "... it was a hybrid, with the mother a polar bear and the father a grizzly," which answers the question.

14. D

Reading through all the choices, B and C can be eliminated right away as they are not mentioned in the text. They might appear as good answers but they are not from the passage.

Looking at choices A and D, the issue is if this has happened before, or has it happened only in zoos. Referring to the text, the second paragraph tells us it is the first hybrid found in the wild.

15. B

Reading through the four choices, the question concerns, what does science know? Does it happen all the time? Completely understood? They do survive? Is it possible? Look in the text for how much is known. The last sentence, "Until 2006, there had been no documented cases of a grizzly polar bear hybrid found in the wild." gives the answer.

Strategy 5 - Elimination

For every question, no matter what type, eliminating obviously incorrect answers narrows the possible choices. Elimination is probably the most powerful strategy for answering multiple-choice.

16. A

Using this strategy the choices can be narrowed down to choices A and D. I have never seen a peacock with red in their tail, so choice C can *probably* be eliminated, but check back. Most birds and many animals have a pattern where the male is colorful and the female less colorful. Choice B can be eliminated as it refers to "both sexes" having colorful tails. Choice D is a good candidate as the text refers to molting season, however, the text does not say how long this is, so there is some doubt. This makes choice A the best choice as it is referred to directly in the text.

17. B

Choice D can be eliminated right away, as a male bird to sit on eggs is not mentioned in the text.

Skimming the passage, choices A and C can be eliminated, as they are not mentioned directly in the text, leaving only choice D.

18. C

Choices A, B and D can be eliminated right away, as the passage states the peacock is the male bird. Referring to the text, "plumage and train of the male peafowl, or peacock ..." making choice C the best choice.

19. D

Choices A and B can be eliminated either right away or with a quick check of the passage, since they are not mentioned. Choice C is suspicious since the grey feathers are under the tail feathers, so it is difficult to see how they could be visible when the tail feathers are lowered.

Strategy 6 - Opposites

If there are opposites, one of them is generally the correct answer. If it helps, make a table that lays out the different options and the correct option will become clear.

20. D

Notice that choices A and D are opposites. Referring to the text, "Smallpox is a highly infectious disease unique to humans ..." eliminates choice A. Also notice choices

B and C are not mentioned in the text and can be eliminated right away.

21. C

Notice that all the choices are opposites. 30% - 35% mortality, or survival rate, or 60%. Therefore, the task is to review the text, looking for 30% or 60%, survival or mortality, stay clear, and do not get confused. Sometimes making notes or a table can help to clarify.

The question is asking about percent, so it is easy and fast to skim the passage for a percent sign.

The first percent sign is in the fourth paragraph, 30% - 35%. Write this in the margin. Next, see what this percent refers to, which is the mortality rate. Write "mortality" next to 30% - 35%. Now, working backwards, see what the 30% - 35% mortality rate refers to. At the beginning of that sentence, is Variola Major.

30% - 35%	Mortality	V. Major

Now we have a clear understanding of what the passage is saying, which we have retrieved quickly and easily, and hopefully will not be confused by the different choices.

Choices A and B can be eliminated right away. Choice C looks correct. Check choice D quickly, and confirm that it is incorrect. Choice C is the correct answer.

22. B

Choices A and B are opposites. Is Variola Minor more or less severe, with more or fewer pox, and more or less scarring? The other two choices, "no pox" and "no treatment" can be eliminated quickly. Either choice A or B are going to be wrong.

Make a quick table like this:

Major - more serious - scars, blindness
Minor - milder

The passage does not mention scarring from Variola minor, but we can infer that it is milder. Looking at the options, choice A is clearly talking about Variola major, and we can infer that choice B is talking about Variola minor and is the correct answer. We can confirm our inference from the text.

Also note the words, 'major' and 'minor.' Which gives a clue concerning severity, and the elimination of choice A.

23. A
Choices A and B are not exactly opposite, but very close and designed to confuse if you do not read them properly. How many people die from the virus? Between 30% and 35%? Or between 35% and 60%? Scan the text with these numbers in mind.

This question is asking about a percent, so quickly scan the passage for a percent sign, which first appears in the second paragraph. Working back, confirm that the percent figures that you quickly found is related to mortality, which it is.

Strategy 7 - Look for Differences

Look at two choices that appear to be correct and examine them carefully.

24. B
Choices A, B and C are very similar and designed to confuse and distract someone who does not look carefully at the text. What is astraphobia exactly? This is a definition question for an unusual word, astraphobia. Scan the text for "astraphobia." Choice B is correct.

25. C
Choices A, B and C are similar and designed to confuse, or tempt a stressed or careless test-taker into making a quick and incorrect choice. Checking the passage, in the first paragraph, lightning occurs in thunderstorms, volcanic eruptions and in dust storms, so choice C is correct.

26. C

All four answers are similar and designed to confuse. Seeing how similar the choices are, it is very important to be clear on the exact definition. Scan the text quickly for the word "fulgurites." From the third paragraph, "This is hot enough to turn sand, some soils or even rock into hollow glass channels..." so the correct answer, and the option that answers the question best, is choice C.

Strategy 8 - Context Clues

Look at the sentences and the context to determine the best option. Sometimes, the answer may be located right in the passage or question.

27. B

You do not have to know the exact meaning - just enough to answer the question. The phrase is used in the passage, "Venus, as the second brightest star in the sky, after the moon, reaches an apparent magnitude of −4.6 ..." where Venus is compared to the brightness of the moon, so the apparent magnitude must have something to do with brightness, which is enough information to answer the question. Notice also, how the choices are opposites. Choice A and B are opposites as are choices C and D.

28. A

The exact meaning is not necessary, you only need only enough information to answer the question. The passage where this phrase is used is, "Venus is an inferior planet from Earth, meaning that it is closer to the sun: its elongation reaches a maximum of 47.8°." Elongation in this sentence is something connected with distance from the sun, but also something to do with Earth. Choice C can be eliminated right away, and since one choice is wrong, Choice D, All of the Above, can also be eliminated. Choice A is the best answer since it mentions, "as seen from earth."

29. A
Choices C and D can be eliminated right away. No mention is made of size or people, so choices C and D are also incorrect. Terrestrial has many similar meanings, but choice A is the best. From the passage, "Venus is one of the four solar terrestrial planets, or rocky bodies that orbit the sun."

Note that choice B is a grammatical error and can be eliminated right away. The question is, "Terrestrial planets are," and choice B is, "Have people on them."

This is a great strategy, looking for grammatical errors and eliminating, and what you might expect to see on a test that a professor has made themselves. However, most standardized tests are generated by computer, and proofed by many different people who have considerable expertise in correcting this type of easy question. Keep this in mind because it is an easy elimination, but don't expect to see this type of thing on a standardized test.

30. A
This is a bit of a trick question and designed to confuse, as it requires an additional step of logical reasoning. Referring to the text, Venus is the *second* closest planet to the sun so there must be one planet that is closer. Planets closer to the sun will rotate the sun faster, so the answer must be choice A.

Strategy 9 - Try out Every Option for Word Meaning Questions

For definition questions, try out all the options - one option will fit better than the rest. As you go through the options, use Strategy 5 - Elimination, to eliminate obviously incorrect choices as you go.

31. B
The answer is taken directly from the passage. Notice that choices A and B are opposites, so one of them will be incorrect. Look in the text carefully for the exact definition. If you are uncertain, make a table in the margin.

Scan the passage looking for the word you are asked to define. Large or unusual words generally stand out and can be located quickly. Once you have found the position in the passage of the word using quick reading scanning techniques, then focus on the sentence and read carefully.

32. B

The sentences talking about the jet stream and monsoons are next to one another. Trying each definition, and comparing to the text, only choice B fits. If you are uncertain, copy the information from the passage into a table.

The question is, what is the relationship between monsoons and the jet stream.

Scan the passage for "jet stream" and "monsoon."

Tropical cyclones	Jet stream
Monsoons and thunderstorms	Different processes

33. D

Referring to the passage, and trying each definition choice, choice D is the only answer that makes sense referring to the text.

34. A

The passage from the text is, "Due to the tilt of the Earth's axis, sunlight reaches the Earth at different angles at different times of the year, creating seasons." Substituting all the choices given into this sentence, slanted, choice A, is the only sensible answer. Here is what substitutions look like:

a. In June the Northern Hemisphere is *slanted* towards the sun...

b. In June the Northern Hemisphere is *rotating* towards the sun...

c. In June the Northern Hemisphere is *connected to* towards the sun...

d. In June the Northern Hemisphere is *bent* towards the sun...

Choice A is the only one that makes sense.

Strategy 10 - You Have to Work for it! Check Carefully for Supporting Details

All answers can be found by carefully reading the text. The questions paraphrase the text found in the passage.

35. C
The passage has a lot of details so read carefully and stay clear.

36. B
The choices are designed to confuse. Check the text for the exact definition and do not be distracted by other choices.

37. A
Here is a quick tip. On choice A, the word hypovolemic is used. This is an unusual word and specific medical vocabulary. None of the other choices uses any specific vocabulary like this, so it is very likely to be the right answer. You can quickly scan the text for this word to confirm. Scanning the text for an unusual word is easy and fast, and one of the most powerful techniques for this type of question.

38. C
Scan the text for Zaire.

Strategy 11 - Look at the Big Picture

Details can be tricky when dealing with main idea and summary questions, but do not let the details distract you. Look at the big picture instead of the smaller parts to determine the right answer.

39. D
The passage says in 2005 it was found there are 3 fruit bat species most suspected of carrying the virus. The details (3 species, fruit bats and 2005) do not matter. Only the fact that bats are suspected.

40. B
The relevant passage is, "Scientists have studied plants, insects and birds as potential reservoir species without success. Bats are the only reservoir species scientists have found." The inference is that these plant and animal species cannot be infected, (i.e. carry and transmit the disease) so choice B is correct.

41. A
The relevant passage is,Apparently, bats are reservoir species for a number of viruses.

Strategy 12 - Make the Best Choice Based on the Information Given

42. D
Choices B and C are incorrect by the passage, "In the early stages, Ebola may not be highly contagious."Choice A is not mentioned, leaving choice D.

43. B
Choices A and D are obviously incorrect and can be eliminated right away. Choice C is irrelevant to the question.

44. A
Choices B and C are not mentioned in the passage. Choice D is a good possibility, however, choice A covers choice D and is referred to in the passage.

45. B
Choice A is incorrect. Choices C and D are not mentioned.

PRACTICE QUESTIONS ANSWER SHEET

	A	B	C	D
1	○	○	○	○
2	○	○	○	○
3	○	○	○	○
4	○	○	○	○
5	○	○	○	○
6	○	○	○	○
7	○	○	○	○
8	○	○	○	○
9	○	○	○	○
10	○	○	○	○
11	○	○	○	○
12	○	○	○	○
13	○	○	○	○

Reading Comprehension Practice

Questions 1 – 4 refer to the following passage.

Passage 1 - Who Was Anne Frank?

You may have heard mention of the word Holocaust in your History or English classes. The Holocaust took place from 1939-1945. It was an attempt by the Nazi party to purify the human race, by eliminating Jews, Gypsies, Catholics, homosexuals and others they deemed inferior to their "perfect" Aryan race. The Nazis used Concentration Camps, which were sometimes used as Death Camps, to exterminate the people they held in the camps. The saddest fact about the Holocaust was the over one million children under the age of sixteen died in a Nazi concentration camp. Just a few weeks before World War II was over, Anne Frank was one of those children to die.

Before the Nazi party began its persecution of the Jews, Anne Frank had a happy life. She was born in June of 1929. In June of 1942, for her 13th birthday, she was given a simple present which would go onto impact the lives of millions of people around the world. That gift was a small red diary that she called Kitty. This diary was to become Anne's most treasured possession when she and her family hid from the Nazis in a secret annex above her father's office building in Amsterdam.

For 25 months, Anne, her sister Margot, her parents, another family, and an elderly Jewish dentist hid from the Nazis in this tiny annex. They were never permitted to go outside, and their food and supplies were brought to them by Miep Gies and her husband, who did not believe in the Nazi persecution of the Jews. It was a very difficult life for young Anne and she used Kitty as an outlet to describe her life in hiding.
After 2 years, Anne and her family were betrayed and arrested by the Nazis. To this day, nobody is exactly sure who betrayed the Frank family and the other annex residents. Anne, her mother, and her sister were separated from Otto Frank, Anne's father. Then, Anne and Margot were separated from their mother. In March of 1945, Margot Frank died of starvation in a Concentration Camp. A few days later, at the age of 15, Anne Frank died of typhus. Of all the people who hid in the Annex, only Otto Frank survived the Holocaust.

Otto Frank returned to the Annex after World War II. It was there that he found Kitty, filled with Anne's thoughts and feelings about being a persecuted Jewish girl. Otto Frank had Anne's diary published in 1947 and it has remained continuously in print ever since. Today, the diary has been published in over 55 languages and more than 24 million copies have been sold around the world. The Diary of Anne Frank tells the story of a brave young woman who tried to see the good in all people.

1. From the context clues in the passage, what does the word Annex mean?

a. Attic

b. Bedroom

c. Basement

d. Kitchen

2. Why do you think Anne's diary has been published in 55 languages?

a. So everyone could understand it.

b. So people around the world could learn more about the horrors of the Holocaust.

c. Because Anne was Jewish but hid in Amsterdam and died in Germany.

d. Because Otto Frank spoke many languages.

3. From the description of Anne and Margot's deaths in the passage, what can we assume typhus is?

a. The same as starving to death.

b. An infection the Germans gave to Anne.

c. A disease Anne caught in the concentration camp.

d. Poison gas used by the Germans to kill Anne.

4. In the third paragraph, what does the word outlet mean?

a. A place to plug things into the wall

b. A store where Miep bought cheap supplies for the Frank family

c. A hiding space similar to an Annex

d. A place where Anne could express her private thoughts.

Questions 5 – 8 refer to the following passage.

Passage 2 - Was Dr. Seuss A Real Doctor?

A favorite author for over 100 years, Theodor Seuss Geisel was born on March 2, 1902. Today, we celebrate the birthday of the famous "Dr. Seuss" by hosting Read Across America events throughout the March. School children around the country celebrate the "Doctor's" birthday by making hats, giving presentations and holding read aloud circles featuring some of Dr. Seuss' most famous books.

But who was Dr. Seuss? Did he go to medical school? Where was his office? You may be surprised to know that Theodor Seuss Geisel was not a medical doctor at all. He took on the nickname Dr. Seuss when he became a noted children's book author. He earned the nickname because people said his books were "as good as medicine." All these years later, his nickname has lasted and he is known as Dr. Seuss all across the world.

Think back to when you were a young child. Did you ever want to try "green eggs and ham?" Did you try to "Hop on Pop?" Do you remember learning about the environment from a creature called The Lorax? Of course, you must recall one of Seuss' most famous characters; that green Grinch who stole Christmas. These stories were all written by Dr. Seuss and featured his signature rhyming words and letters. They also featured made up words to enhance his rhyme scheme and even though many of his characters were made up, they sure seem real to us today.

And what of his "signature" book, The Cat in the Hat? You must remember that cat and Thing One and Thing Two from your childhood. Did you know that in the early 1950's there was a growing concern in America that children were not becoming avid readers? This was, book publishers thought, because children found books dull and uninteresting. An intelligent publisher sent Dr. Seuss a book of words that he thought all children should learn as young readers. Dr. Seuss wrote his famous story The Cat in the Hat, using those words. We can see, over the decades, just how much influence his writing has had on very young children. That is why we celebrate this doctor's birthday each March.

5. What does the word "avid" mean in the last paragraph?

a. Good
b. Interested
c. Slow
d. Fast

6. What can we infer from the statement " His books were like medicine?"

a. His books made people feel better
b. His books were in doctor's office waiting rooms
c. His books took away fevers
d. His books left a funny taste in readers' mouths.

7. Why is the publisher in the last paragraph called "intelligent?"

a. The publisher knew how to read.
b. The publisher knew kids did not like to read.
c. The publisher knew Dr. Seuss would be able to create a book that sold well.
d. The publisher knew that Dr. Seuss would be able to write a book that would get young children interested in reading.

8. The theme of this passage is

a. Dr. Seuss was not a doctor.
b. Dr. Seuss influenced the lives of generations of young children.
c. Dr. Seuss wrote rhyming books.
d. Dr. Suess' birthday is a good day to read a book.

Questions 9 - 13 refer to the following passage.

Accident in the Workplace

Construction is one of the biggest industrial sectors in any country. The construction industry plays an important role in the development of a nation as well as in supporting the economy. However, the risks on a construction site are remarkably high. On the other hand, numerous preventive measures minimize the risks. Accidents happen frequently every year with many people losing their lives and becoming seriously injured.

Most accidents occur when cleaning equipment or machinery. For example, a recent incident occurred on a construction site in which an 18-year-old worker lost his life when getting entangled in portable mortar mixer. The worker was cleaning of mixer at the completion of his shift, to prepare it for the next day. He neglected the safety protocols and did not turn off the supply of mixer before starting the maintenance.

After a while, a painter working nearby heard him. He immediately rushed over and found the worker's arm was stuck in the mixer and he was being pulled into rotating mixer paddles. First the painter tried to pull his arm out of the mixer but not able to. Next, he tried to cut off the power supply, but it was too late.

He was unable to disengage the gears and started yelling for help from his co-workers nearby. A coworker heard and ran towards the machine and immediately shut it off.

As soon as the incident was reported, management acted quickly and called the emergency medical services. Emergency services reached the workplace within next 10 minutes due to the accident severity and seriousness. Rescue workers dismantled the machine and reversed the paddles to free the stuck worker. However, the worker was found dead at the scene of incidence.

The employer was partly to blame as they neglected to professionally train employees in the appropriate safety procedures, namely, that the equipment must be shut down and disconnected from the power source. Here the worker also neglected the maintenance procedures and began maintenance when it was fully operational. As a result, he paid with his life.

Safety in the workplace is the responsibility of employer as well as the employees. Machine parts, where there is higher risk of injuries, must be covered with the safety shields/ guards. Warning signs must be displayed in high-risk locations. Workers must be trained in safety procedures and emergency situations. Only then can tragic accidents like this be avoided.

9. What type of activities are carried out on a construction site?

a. High Risk Activities
b. Mild Risk Activities
c. Low Risk Activities
d. No Risk involved

10. What was the cause of this incident?

a. Management Policies
b. Personal Negligence
c. Management Negligence
d. Both a, b, and c

11. Why was management negligent in this accident?

a. Lack of employee training
b. No health and safety inspector on site
c. No instructions displayed near the workstation/ workplace.
d. All of the above

12. Which type of management approach is described in this passage?

a. Proactive
b. Reactive

13. What steps do you think management should take to reduce workplace accidents?

a. Hire safety supervisors
b. Do nothing
c. Fire the current workers and hire new ones
d. Shut down the unit and project activities

ANSWER KEY

1. A
We know that an annex is like an attic because the text states the annex was above Otto Frank's building.

Choice B is incorrect because an office building doesn't have bedrooms. Choice C is incorrect because a basement would be below the office building. Choice D is incorrect because there would not be a kitchen in an office building.

2. B
The diary has been published in 55 languages so people all over the world can learn about Anne. That is why the passage says it has been continuously in print.

Choice A is incorrect because it is too vague. Choice C is incorrect because it was published after Anne died and she did not write in all three languages. Choice D is incorrect because the passage does not give us any information about what languages Otto Frank spoke.

3. C
Use the process of elimination to figure this out.

Choice A cannot be the correct answer because, otherwise the passage would have simply said that Anne and Margot both died of starvation. Choices B and D cannot be correct because, if the Germans had done something specifically to murder Anne, the passage would have stated that directly. By the process of elimination, choice C has to be the correct answer.

4. D
We can figure this out using context clues. The paragraph is talking about Anne's diary and so, outlet in this instance is a place where Anne can pour her feelings.

Choice A is incorrect answer. That is the literal meaning of the word outlet and the passage is using the figurative meaning. Choice B is incorrect because that is the secondary literal meaning of the word outlet, as in an outlet mall. Again, we are looking for figurative meaning. Choice C is incorrect because there are no clues in the text to support that answer.

5. B
When someone is avid about something that means they are highly interested in the subject. The context clues are dull and boring, because they define the opposite of avid.

6. A
The author is using a simile to compare the books to medicine. Medicine is what you take when you want to feel better. They are suggesting that if you want to feel good, they should read Dr. Seuss' books.

Choice B is incorrect because there is no mention of a doctor's office. Choice C is incorrect because it is using the literal meaning of medicine and the author is using medicine in a figurative way. Choice D is incorrect because it makes no sense. We know not to eat books.

7. D
The publisher is described as intelligent because he knew to get in touch with a famous author to develop a book that children would be interested in reading.

Choice A is incorrect because we can assume that all book publishers must know how to read. Choice B is incorrect because it says in the article that more than one publisher was concerned whether children liked to read. Choice D is incorrect because there is no mention in the article about how well The Cat in the Hat sold when it was first published.

8. B
The passage describes in detail how Dr. Seuss had a great effect on the lives of children through his writing. It names several of his books, tells how he helped children become avid readers and explains his style of writing.

Choice A is incorrect because that is just one single fact

about the passage. Choice C is incorrect because that is just one single fact about the passage. Choice D is incorrect because that is just one single fact about the passage. Again, choice B is correct because it encompasses ALL the facts in the passage, not just one single fact.

9. A

Choice A is correct because of large number of accidents occur on construction sites.

10. D

Choice D is correct because management as well as the employee are responsible for this accident.
Choice A is incorrect because the employee was also responsible
Choice B is incorrect because management was also responsible
Choice C is incorrect because management cannot be blamed solely for this accident.

11. D

Choice D is correct because all the three mentioned precautionary measures must be taken by the management.

12. B

Choice A is incorrect because before the incident no action has been taken by the management.
Choice B is correct because management took serious action after the occurrence of accident.

13. A

Choice A is correct because safety professionals are expert in health and safety issues present in the workplace. They can easily identify as well as rectify the problems.
Choice B is incorrect and can be eliminated right away. Continuous improvement is important for companies to grow and excel in their fields.
Choice C is irrelevant and can be eliminated right away
Choice D is not suitable because shutting down of the project is not a good option at all.

Basic Math Multiple-Choice Strategy

How to Answer Basic Math Questions - the Basics

First, read the problem, but not the answers.

Work through the problem first and come up with your own answers. Hopefully, you should find your answer among the choices.

If no answer matches the one you got, re-check your math, but this time, use a different method. In math, there are different ways to solve a problem.

Math Multiple Choice Strategy

The two strategies for working with basic math multiple choice are Estimation and Elimination.

Estimation is just as it sounds - try to estimate an approximate answer first. Then look at the choices.

Elimination is probably the most powerful strategy for answering multiple choice.

Eliminate obviously incorrect answers and narrowing the possible choices.

Here are a few basic math examples of how this works.

Solve 2/3 + 5/12

a. 9/17
b. 3/11
c. 7/12
d. 1 1/12

First estimate the answer. 2/3 is more than half and 5/12 is about half, so the answer is going to be very close to 1.

Next, Eliminate. Choice A is about 1/2 and can be eliminated, choice B is very small, less than 1/2 and can be eliminated. Choice C is close to 1/2 and can be eliminated. Leaving only choice D, which is just over 1.

Work through the solution, find a common denominator and add. The correct answer is 1 1/12, so Choice D is correct.

Let's look at another example:

Solve 4/5 – 2/3

a. 2/2
b. 2/13
c. 1
d. 2/15

First, quickly estimate the answer. 4/5 is very close to 1, and 2/3 more than half, so the answer is going to be less than 1/2.

Choice A can be eliminated right away, because it is 1. Choice C can be eliminated for the same reason.

Next, look at the denominators. Since 5 and 3 don't go into 13, choice B can be eliminated as well. That leaves choice D. Checking the answer, the common denominator will be 15. So the answer is 2/15 and choice D is correct.

Answer Sheet

	A	B	C	D
1	○	○	○	○
2	○	○	○	○
3	○	○	○	○
4	○	○	○	○
5	○	○	○	○
6	○	○	○	○
7	○	○	○	○
8	○	○	○	○
9	○	○	○	○
10	○	○	○	○

Basic Math Strategy Practice Questions

1. 3/5 ÷ 4/5

a. 12/5
b. 3/4
c. 2 2/5
d. 1 1/5

2. 2/9 ÷ 4/9

a. 3/4
b. 3/9
c. 1 1/9
d. 1/2

3. Solve 2/3 + 5/12

a. 9/17
b. 3/11
c. 7/12
d. 1 1/12

4. 7/11 + 3/11

a. 6/11
b. 9/11
c. 10/11
d. 4/11

5. 13/15 – 7/15

a. 3/5
b. 7/15
c. 2/5
d. 6

6. 6/10 x 5/16

a. 4/15
b. 3/16
c. 2 1/3
d. 2/7

7. 7.25 x 0.5

a. 3.625
b. 3.526
c. 36.25
d. 35.25

8. 6.363 - 1.602

a. 4.011
b. 4.761
c. 47.61
d. 3.761

9. 3.57 - 3.21

a. 03.6
b. 0.036
c. 0.36
d. 0.136

10. 67.54 – 43.45

a. 24.09

a. 24.19

a. C 24.019

a. D 23.09

Answer Key

1. B
3/5 x 5/4 = 3/1 x 1/4 = ¾

Choice A, C, and D can be eliminated as they are too high to be the answer.

2. D
2/9 x 9/4 = 2/1 x ¼ = 2/4 = ½

Choice C can be eliminated as it is too high to be the answer. Since you multiply the inverse, the denominator would not be 9. And since you could estimate that it'd be closer to ½ than ¾, so choice A can be eliminated as well.

3. D
A common denominator is needed, a number which both 3 and 12 will divide into. So, 8+5/12 = 13/12 = 1 1/12

You know that since 2/3 is almost a whole number, that Choice B 3/11 is out, since it is close to 0.

You can immediately eliminate Choice A because since you need to find the common denominator, neither 3 or 12 goes in to 17 evenly.

You can narrow it down to Choice C and Choice D. But once you figure out the common denominator, it being 12, you can arrive at D, since 7 is the sum of 2 and 5, and you know one of them needs to be changed due to the common denominator.

4. C
Since the denominators are the same, we can just add the numerators, so 7+3/11 = 10/11

Since 4, 6, and 9 are all less than the sum of 7 + 3, you can eliminate Choice A, B, and D.

5. C
Since the denominators are the same, we can just subtract the numerators, so 13-7/15 = 6/15 = 2/5

You can eliminate Choice D because it is a whole number. Since Choice B is the same as one of the fractions in the problem, you can eliminate that, since subtracting it is not going to equal one of the numbers in the problem.

6. B
Since there are common numerators and denominators to cancel out, we cancel out 6/10 x 5/16 to get 6/2 x 1/16 = 3/2 x 1/8, and then we multiply numerators and denominators to get 3/16

Choice C can be eliminated because multiplying fractions does not give whole numbers. 15 and 7 are not common denominators with 10 or 16, so A and D can be eliminated as well.

7. A
7.25 x 0.5 = 3.625
Since the rule is you want to have as many numbers behind the decimal place in the answer as the sum of the ones in the initial problem, Choice C and D are eliminated. Since it's a multiple of 5, the last number would be 5 and not 6, eliminating Choice B.

8. B
6.363 - 1.602 = 4.761

Choice C can be eliminated as it is larger than the starting numbers. 1.602 is about half of 3, so you can eliminate D for being too small of a number.

9. C
3.57 - 3.21 = 0.36

Choice A can be eliminated as it is a larger number than both of the starting numbers. Choice B and D have too many places after the decimal point, so they can be eliminated.

10. A
67.54 – 43.45 = 24.09

Choice C can be eliminated because there are too many numbers after the decimal place.

Basic math Video Tutorials

https://www.test-preparation.ca/math-videos/

Fraction Tips, Tricks and Shortcuts

When you are writing an exam, time is precious, so anything you can do to answer questions faster is a real advantage.

Here are some ideas, shortcuts, tips and tricks that can speed up answering fraction problems.

Remember that a fraction is just a number which names a portion of something. For instance, instead of having a whole pie, a fraction says you have a part of a pie--such as a half of one or a fourth of one.

Two numbers make up a fraction. The number on top is the numerator. The number on the bottom is the denominator.

To remember which is which, just remember that "denominator" and "down" both start with a "d." And the "downstairs" number is the denominator. So for instance, in ½, the numerator is 1, and the denominator (or "downstairs") number is 2.

Adding Fractions

It's easy to add two fractions if they have the same denominator. Just add the digits on top and leave the bottom one the same: 1/10 + 6/10 = 7/10.

It's the same with subtracting fractions with the same denominator: 7/10 - 6/10 = 1/10.

Adding and subtracting fractions with different denominators is a little more complicated.

First, you have to arrange the fractions so they have the same denominators.

The easiest way to do this is to multiply the denominators: For 2/5 + 1/2 multiply 5 by 2. Now you have a denominator of 10.

But now you have to change the top numbers too. Since you multiplied the 5 in 2/5 by 2, you also multiply the 2 by 2, to get 4. So the first fraction is now 4/10.

In the second fraction, you multiplied the denominator by 5, you have to multiply the numerator by 5 also, to get 5/10.

Now you have 4/10 + 5/10 and you can add 5 and 4 to get 9/10.

Simplest Form

To reduce a fraction to its simplest form, you have to arrange the numerator and denominator so the only common factor is 1.

Think of it this way:

Let's take an example: The fraction 2/10.

This is not reduced to its simplest terms because there is a number that will divide evenly into both: 2. We want to make it so that the only number that will divide evenly into both is 1.

Divide the top and bottom by 2 to get the new, reduced fraction - 1/5.

Multiplying Fractions

This is the easiest of all: Just multiply the two top numbers and then multiply the two bottom numbers.

Here is an example,

2/5 X 2/3

First, multiply the numerators: 2 X 2 = 4

then multiply the denominators: 5 X 3 = 15

Your answer is 4/15.

Dividing Fractions

Dividing fractions is easy if you remember a simple trick - first turn the second fraction upside down - then multiply!

Here is an example:

7/8 X 1/2

Turn the second fraction upside down:

7/8 X 2/1

then multiply:

(7 X 2) / (8 X 1) = 14/8

Converting Fractions to Decimals

There are a couple of ways to convert fractions to decimals. The first, which is the fastest -- is to memorize some basic fraction facts.

> 1/100 is “one hundredth,” expressed as a decimal, it’s .01.
>
> 1/50 is “two hundredths,” expressed as a decimal, it’s .02.
>
> 1/25 is “one twenty-fifth” or “four hundredths,” expressed as a decimal, it’s .04.
>
> 1/20 is “one twentieth” or “”five hundredths,” expressed as a decimal, it’s .05.

1/10 is "one tenth," expressed as a decimal, it's .1.

1/8 is "one eighth," or "one hundred twenty-five thousandths," expressed as a decimal, it's .125.

1/5 is "one fifth," or "two tenths," expressed as a decimal, it's .2.

1/4 is "one fourth" or "twenty-five hundredths," expressed as a decimal, it's .25.

1/3 is "one third" or "thirty-three hundredths," expressed as a decimal, it's .33.

1/2 is "one half" or "five tenths," expressed as a decimal, it's .5.

3/4 is "three fourths," or "seventy-five hundredths," expressed as a decimal, it's .75.

Of course, if you're no good at memorization, another good technique for converting a fraction to a decimal is to manipulate it so that the fraction's denominator is 10, 100, 1000, or some other power of 10.

Here's an example: We'll start with three quarters. What is the first number in the 4 "times table" that you can multiply and get a multiple of 10? Can you multiply 4 by something to get 10? No. Can you multiply it by something to get 100? Yes! 4 X 25 is 100.

So multiply the numerator by 25, which is 75 over 100

We know fractions are really a division problem, and we also know that dividing by 100, means we move the decimal 2 places to the left.

So, 75 over 100 = .75

Lets try another example - Convert one fifth to a decimal.

First find a power of 10 that 5 goes into evenly, which is 2.

Multiply the numerator and denominator by 2, which is

two tenths.

Dividing 2 by 10 means we move the decimal place 1 place to the left.

So 1/5 = 0.5

Converting Fractions to Percent

Here is a quick method to convert fraction to percent and a strategy for answering on a multiple choice test that will save you valuable exam time.

First, remember that a fraction is a division problem: you're dividing the bottom number into the top.

Taking an example, convert 2/3 into percent.

The first method is to multiple the numerator by 100 and divide. So,

(2 X 100) / 2 = 100/3 = 66.66

Add a % sign and you have the answer, 66.66%

If you're doing these conversions on a multiple-choice test, here's an idea that might be even easier and faster. Let's say you have a fraction of 1/8 and you're asked to convert to percent.

Since we know that "percent" means hundredths, ask yourself what number we can multiply 8 by to get 100. Since there is no number, ask what number gets us close to 100.

That number is 12: 8 X 12 = 96. So it gets us a little less than 100. Now, whatever you do to the denominator, you have to do to the numerator. Let's multiply 1 X 12 and we get 12. However, since 96 is a little less than 100, we know that our answer will be a little MORE than 12%.

Look at the choices and eliminate the obvious wrong choices. So if your possible answers on the multiple-choice test are these:

a) 8.5% b) 19% c)12.5% d) 25%

then we know the answer is c) 12.5%, because it's a little MORE than the 12 we got in our math problem above.

Here all the choices except choice C 12.5% can be eliminated.

You don't have to know the exact correct answer, just enough to estimate, then eliminate the obviously wrong answers.

This was an easy example to demonstrate the strategy, but don't be fooled! You probably won't get such an easy question on your exam. By estimating your answer quickly, then eliminating obviously incorrect choices immediately, you save precious exam time.

Decimal Tips, Tricks and Shortcuts

Converting Decimals to Fractions

Converting decimals to fractions is easy if you say it the right way! If you say "point one" or "point 25," you'll have trouble.

But if you say, "one tenth" and "twenty-five hundredths," then you have already solved it! That's because, if you know your fractions, you know that "one tenth" looks like this: 1/10. And "twenty-five hundredths" looks like this: 25/100.

Even if you have digits before the decimal, such as 3.4, learning how to say the word will help you with the conversion into a fraction. It's not "three point four," it's "three and four tenths." Knowing this, you know that the fraction which looks like “three and four tenths” is 3 4/10.

The conversion is not complete until you reduce the fraction to its lowest terms: It’s not 25/100, but 1/4.

Converting Decimals to Percent

Changing a decimal to a percent is easy if you remember one thing: multiply by 100.

For example, if you start with .45, simply multiply it by 100 for 45. Then add the % sign to the end - 45%.

Think of it this way: take out the decimal point, add a percent sign on the opposite side. In other words, the decimal on the left is replaced by the % on the right.

It doesn’t work quite that easily if the decimal is in the middle of the number. For example, 3.7. Here, take out the decimal in the middle and replace it with a 0 % at the end. So 3.7 converted to decimal is 370%.

Percent Tips, Tricks and Shortcuts

Percent problems are not nearly as scary as they appear, if you remember this neat trick:

Draw a cross as in:

Portion	Percent
Whole	100

In the upper left, write PORTION. In the bottom left write WHOLE. In the top right, write PERCENT and in the bottom right, write 100. Whatever your problem is, you will leave blank the unknown, and fill in the other four parts. For example, let's suppose your problem is: Find 10% of 50. Since we know the 10% part, we put 10 in the percent corner. Since the whole number in our problem is 50, we put that in the corner marked whole. You always put 100 underneath the percent, so we leave it as is, which leaves only the top left corner blank. This is where we'll put our answer. Now simply multiply the two corner numbers that are NOT 100. Here, it's 10 X 50. That gives us 500. Now divide this by the remaining corner, or 100, to get a final answer of 5. 5 is the number that goes in the upper-left corner, and is your final solution.

Another hint to remember: Percents are the same thing as hundredths in decimals. So .45 is the same as 45 hundredths or 45 percent.

Converting Percents to Decimals

Percents are just a type of decimal, so it should be no surprise that converting between the two is actually fairly simple. Here are a few tricks and shortcuts to keep in mind:

- Remember that percent literally means "per 100" or "for every 100." So when you speak of 30% you're saying 30 for every 100 or the fraction 30/100. In basic math, you learned that fractions that have 10 or 100 as the denominator can easily be turned to a decimal. 30/100 is thirty hundredths, or expressed as a decimal, .30.
- Another way to look at it: To convert a percent to a decimal, simply divide the number by 100. So for instance, if the percent is 47%, divide 47 by 100. The result will be .47. Get rid of the % mark and you're done.
- Remember that the easiest way of dividing by 100 is by moving your decimal two spots to the left.

Converting Percents to Fractions

Converting percents to fractions is easy. After all, a percent is just a type of fraction; it tells you what part of 100 that you're talking about. Here are some simple ideas for making the conversion from a percent to a fraction:

- If the percent is a whole number -- say 34% -- then simply write a fraction with 100 as the denominator (the bottom number). Then put the percentage itself on top. So 34% becomes 34/100.
- Now reduce as you would reduce any percent. In this case, by dividing 2 into 34 and 2 into 100, you get 17/50.
- If your percent is not a whole number -- say 3.4% --then convert it to a decimal expressed as hundredths. 3.4 is the same as 3.40 (or 3 and forty hundredths). Now ask yourself how you would express "three and forty hundredths" as a fraction. It would, of course, be 3 40/100. Reduce this and it becomes 3 2/5.

Word Problem Multiple-Choice Strategy

How to Solve Word Problems

https://www.youtube.com/watch?v=GY2urix31jo

Do you know what the biggest tip for solving word problems is?

Practice regularly and systematically.

Sounds simple and easy right? Yes it is, and yes it really does work.

Word problems are a way of thinking and require you to translate a real-world problem into mathematical terms.

Some math teachers say that learning how to think mathematically is the main reason for teaching word problems.

So what does that mean?

Studying word problems and math in general requires a logical and mathematical frame of mind. The only way you can get this is by practicing regularly, which means every day.

It is critical that you practice word problems every day for the 5 days before the exam as the absolute minimum.

If you practice and miss a day, you have lost the mathematical frame of mind and the benefit of your previous practice is gone. You must start all over again.

Everything is important.

All the information given in the problem has some purpose. There is no unnecessary information! Word problems are typically around 50 words in 2 or 3 sentences.

Often, the relationships are complicated. To explain everything, every word counts.

Make sure that you use every piece of information.

7 STEPS TO SOLVING WORD PROBLEMS

Step 1 – Read through the problem at least three times. The first reading should be a quick scan, and the next two readings should be done slowly to find answers to these questions:

> What does the problem ask? (Usually located at the end)

Mark all information and underline all important words or phrases.

Step 2 – Draw a picture. Use arrows, circles, lines, whatever works for you. This makes the problem real.

A favorite word problem is something like, 1 train leaves Station A travelling at 100 km/hr and another train leaves Station B travelling at 60 km/hr. ...

Draw a line, the two stations, and the two trains at either end.

Depending on the question, make a table with a blank portion to show information you don't know.

Step 3 – Assign a single letter to represent each unknown.

You may want to note the unknown that each letter represents so you don't get confused.

Step 4 – Translate the information into an equation.

Remember that the main problem with word problems is that they are not expressed in regular math equations. Your ability to identify correctly the variables and translate the information into an equation determines your ability to solve the problem.

Step 5 – Check the equation to see if it looks like regular equations that you are used to seeing and whether it looks sensible.

Does the equation appear to represent the information in the question? Take note that you may need to rewrite some formulas needed to solve the word problem equation.

Step 6 – Use algebra rules to solve the equation.

Simplify each side of the equation by removing parentheses and combining like terms.

Use addition or subtraction to isolate the variable term on one side of the equation. If a number crosses to the other side of the equation, the sign changes to the opposite -- for example positive to negative.

Use multiplication or division to solve for the variable. What you to once side of the equation you must do for the other.

Where there are multiple unknowns you will need to use elimination or substitution methods to resolve all the equations.

Step 7 – Check your final answers to see if they make sense with the information given in the problem.

For example, if the word problem involves a discount, the final price should be less or if a product was taxed then the final answer has to cost more.

Types of Word problems

Word problems can be classified into 12 types. Below are examples of each type with a complete solution. Some types of Word problems can be solved quickly using multiple-choice strategies and some cannot. Always look for ways to estimate the answer and then eliminate choices.

1. Age

A girl is 10 years older than her brother. By next year, she will be twice the age of her brother. What are their ages now?

a. 25, 15
b. 19, 9
c. 21, 11
d. 29, 19

Solution: B

We will assume that the girl's age is "a" and her brother's is "b." This means that based on the information in the first sentence,
$a = 10$

Next year, she will be twice her brother's age, which gives
$a + 1 = 2(b+1)$

We need to solve for one unknown factor and then use the answer to solve for the other. To do this we substitute the value of "a" from the first equation into the second equation. This gives

$10+b + 1 = 2b + 2$
$11 + b = 2b + 2$
$11 - 2 = 2b - b$
$b= 9$

$9 = b$ this means that her brother is 9 years old.
Solving for the girl's age in the first equation gives

a = 10 + 9
a = 19 the girl is aged 19. So, the girl is aged 19 and the boy is 9

2. Distance or speed

Two boats travel down a river towards the same destination, starting at the same time. One boat is traveling at 52 km/hr, and the other boat at 43 km/hr. How far apart will they be after 40 minutes?

a. 46.67 km
b. 19.23 km
c. 6.03 km
d. 14.39 km

Solution: C

After 40 minutes, the first boat will have traveled = 52 km/hr x 40 minutes/60 minutes = 34.7 km

After 40 minutes, the second boat will have traveled = 43 km/hr x 40/60 minutes = 28.66 km

Difference between the two boats will be 34.7 km – 28.66 km = 6.03 km

Multiple-Choice Strategy

First estimate the answer. The first boat is travelling 9 km. faster than the second, for 40 minutes, which is 2/3 of an hour. 2/3 of 9 = 6, as a rough guess of the distance apart.

Choices A, B and D can be eliminated right away.

3. Ratio

The instructions in a cookbook states that 700 grams of flour must be mixed in 100 ml of water, and 0.90 grams of salt added. A cook however has just 325 grams of flour. What is the quantity of water and salt that he should use?

a. 0.41 grams and 46.4 ml
b. 0.45 grams and 49.3 ml
c. 0.39 grams and 39.8 ml
d. 0.25 grams and 40.1 ml

Solution: A

The Cookbook states 700 grams of flour, but the cook only has 325. The first step is to determine the percentage of flour he has 325/700 x 100 = 46.4%
That means that 46.4% of all other items must also be used.
46.4% of 100 = 46.4 ml of water
46.4% of 0.90 = 0.41 grams of salt.

Multiple-Choice Strategy

The recipe calls for 700 grams of flour but the cook only has 325, which is just less than half, the amount of water and salt are going to be about half.

Choices C and D can be eliminated right away. Choice B is very close so be careful. Looking closely at Choice B, it is exactly half, and since 325 is slightly less than half of 700, it can't be correct.

Choice A is correct.

4. Percent

An agent received $6,685 as his commission for selling a property. If his commission was 13% of the selling price, how much was the property?

a. $68,825
b. $121,850
c. $49,025
d. $51,423

Solution: D

Let's assume that the property price is x
That means from the information given, 13% of x = 6,685

Solve for x,
x = 6685 x 100/13 = $51,423

Multiple-Choice Strategy

The commission,13%, is just over 10%, which is easier to work with. Round up $6685 to $6700, and multiple by 10 for an approximate answer. 10 X 6700 = $67,000. You can do this in your head. Choice B is much too big and can be eliminated. Choice C is too small and can be eliminated. Choices A and D are left and good possibilities.
Do the calculations to make the final choice.

5. Sales & Profit

A store owner buys merchandise for $21,045. He transports them for $3,905 and pays his staff $1,450 to stock the merchandise on his shelves. If he does not incur further costs, how much does he need to sell the items to make $5,000 profit?

a. $32,500
b. $29,350
c. $32,400
d. $31,400

Solution: D

Total cost of the items is $21,045 + $3,905 + $1,450 = $26,400
Total cost is now $26,400 + $5000 profit = $31,400

Multiple-Choice Strategy

Round off and add the numbers up in your head quickly. 21,000 + 4,000 + 1500 = 26500. Add in 5000 profit for a total of 31500.

Choice B is too small and can be eliminated. Choice C and Choice A are too large and can be eliminated.

6. Tax/Income

A woman earns $42,000 per month and pays 5% tax on her monthly income. If the Government increases her monthly taxes by $1,500, what is her income after tax?

a. $38,400
b. $36,050
c. $40,500
d. $39, 500

Solution: A

Initial tax on income was 5/100 x 42,000 = $2,100
$1,500 was added to the tax to give $2,100 + 1,500 = $3,600
Income after tax left is $42,000 - $3,600 = $38,400

7. Interest

A man invests $3000 in a 2-year term deposit that pays 3% interest per year. How much will he have at the end of the 2-year term?

a. $5,200
b. $3,020
c. $3,182.7
d. $3,000

Solution: C

This is a compound interest problem. The funds are invested for 2 years and interest is paid yearly, so in the second year, he will earn interest on the interest paid in the first year.

3% interest in the first year = 3/100 x 3,000 = $90
At end of first year, total amount = 3,000 + 90 = $3,090
Second year = 3/100 x 3,090 = 92.7.
At end of second year, total amount = $3090 + $92.7 = $3,182.7

8. Averaging

The average weight of 10 books is 54 grams. 2 more books were added and the average weight became 55.4. If one of the 2 new books added weighed 62.8 g, what is the weight of the other?

a. 44.7 g
b. 67.4 g
c. 62 g
d. 52 g

Solution: C

Total weight of 10 books with average 54 grams will be=10×54=540 g
Total weight of 12 books with average 55.4 will be=55.4×12=664.8 g
So total weight of the remaining 2 will be= 664.8 – 540 = 124.8 g
If one weighs 62.8, the weight of the other will be= 124.8 g – 62.8 g = 62 g

Multiple-Choice Strategy

Averaging problems can be estimated by looking at which direction the average goes. If additional items are added and the average goes up, the new items much be greater than the average. If the average goes down after new items are added, the new items must be less than the average.

Here, the average is 54 grams and 2 books are added which increases the average to 55.4, so the new books must weight more than 54 grams.

Choices A and D can be eliminated right away.

9. Probability

A bag contains 15 marbles of various colors. If 3 marbles are white, 5 are red and the rest are black, what is the probability of randomly picking out a black marble from the bag?

a. 7/15
b. 3/15
c. 1/5
d. 4/15

Solution: A

Total marbles = 15
Number of black marbles = 15 – (3 + 5) = 7
Probability of picking out a black marble = 7/15

10. Two Variables

A company paid a total of $2850 to book for 6 single rooms and 4 double rooms in a hotel for one night. Another company paid $3185 to book for 13 single rooms for one night in the same hotel. What is the cost for single and double rooms in that hotel?

a. single= $250 and double = $345
b. single= $254 and double = $350
c. single = $245 and double = $305
d. single = $245 and double = $345

Solution: D

We can determine the price of single rooms from the information given of the second company. 13 single rooms = 3185.
One single room = 3185 / 13 = 245
The first company paid for 6 single rooms at $245. 245 x 6 = $1470
Total amount paid for 4 double rooms by first company = $2850 - $1470 = $1380
Cost per double room = 1380 / 4 = $345

11. Geometry

The length of a rectangle is 5 in. more than its width. The perimeter of the rectangle is 26 in. What is the width and length of the rectangle?

a. width = 6 inches, Length = 9 inches
b. width = 4 inches, Length = 9 inches
c. width =4 inches, Length = 5 inches
d. width = 6 inches, Length = 11 inches

Solution: B

Formula for perimeter of a rectangle is 2(L + W)
p=26, so 2(L+W) = p
The length is 5 inches more than the width, so
2(w + 5) + 2w = 26
2w + 10 + 2w = 26
2w + 2w = 26 - 10
4w = 16

W = 16/4 = 4 inches

L is 5 inches more than w, so L = 5 + 4 = 9 inches.

12. Totals and fractions

A basket contains 125 oranges, mangos and apples. If 3/5 of the fruits in the basket are mangos and only 2/5 of the mangos are ripe, how many ripe mangos are there in the basket?

a. 30
b. 68
c. 55
d. 47

Solution: A
Number of mangos in the basket is 3/5 x 125 = 75
Number of ripe mangos = 2/5 x 75 = 30

Practice and Video Tutorial

https://www.test-preparation.ca/word-problem/

Answer Sheet

	A	B	C	D
1	○	○	○	○
2	○	○	○	○
3	○	○	○	○
4	○	○	○	○
5	○	○	○	○
6	○	○	○	○
7	○	○	○	○
8	○	○	○	○
9	○	○	○	○
10	○	○	○	○

Practice Questions

1. A motorcycle is traveling at 100 km/hr. How far will it travel in 2 minutes?

a. 1.6
b. 3.3
c. 1
d. 12.5

2. Bill invests $4,000 at 8% compounded yearly. How much will he have in 2 years?

a. $4320.00
b. $4665.60
c. $4640.00
d. $4800.00

3. A waitress serves 10 tables one evening on her shift from 6 - 12:00 PM. She makes $10.50 per hour plus tips. Her total bills come to $240.60 with an average tip of 12%. How much did she make?

a. $28.87
b. $63.00
c. $91.87
d. $81.87

4. The cost of waterproofing canvas is .50 a square yard. What's the total cost for waterproofing a canvas truck cover that is 15' x 24'?

a. $18.00
b. $6.67
c. $180.00
d. $20.00

5. John is a barber and receives 40% of the amount paid by each of his customers, and all of any tips paid to him. If a man pays $8.50 for a haircut and tips $1.30, how much money does John receive?

a. $3.92
b. $4.70
c. $5.70
d. $6.40

6. Two trains start their journey at the same time, one with average speed of 72 km/hr and other with 52 km/hr. How far apart are the trains after 20 minutes?

a. 6.67 km
b. 17.33 km
c. 24.3 km
d. 41.33 km

7. John purchased a jacket at a 7% discount. He had a membership and received an additional discount of 1.6%. If he paid $425, what is the retail price of the jacket?

a. $448
b. $460
c. $466
d. $472

8. A store sells stereos for $545. If 15% of the cost was added to the price as value added tax, what is the total cost?

a. $490.4
b. $626.75
c. $575.00
d. $590.15

9. A car covers a certain distance in 3.5 hours at an average speed of 60 km/hr. How much time in hours will a motorbike take to cover the same distance at an average speed of 40 km/hr?

a. 4.5
b. 4.75
c. 5.25
d. 5

10. Jim left home for the office at 7:00 am. He reached his office at 7:48 am. How far is his house from office if his average driving speed is 40km/hr?

a. 32 km
b. 34 km
c. 38 km
d. 40 km

Answer Key

1. B
First calculate the distance traveled in 1 minute.
100 km/hr. = 100/60 = 1.666 km/minute.
So, in 2 minutes the motorcycle will travel 3.33 kilometers.

2. B
For the first year, $4,000 invested at 8% will be 4000 X .08 = 320. The interest is compounded yearly, so to calculate the second years interest, 4320 X .08 = 345.60. The total will then be 4320 + 345.60 = $4665.60

3. C
First calculate her hourly wage. 6 hours X 10.50/hour = $63. Next calculate tips. $240.60 X .12 = $28.87. So her total earnings will be 63 + 28.87 = 91.87

4. C
This is a square foot cost problem. The problem is to find the total square footage, and the multiply by the cost.

Use math shortcuts to calculate the answer in your head. First calculate total square feet, which is 15 * 24 = 360 ft^2. Next, convert this value to square yards, (1 $yards^2$ = 9 ft^2) which is 360/9 = 40 $yards^2$. At $0.50 per square yard, the total cost is 40 * 0.50 (or half) = $20.

This is actually the correct answer choice D.

5. B
Estimate the answer in your head quickly. 40% is close to 50%, which is half. 50% of $8.50 is 4.25 plus tips of $1.30 is 5.55 approximately.

Looking at the options, choices A and D can all be eliminated as too low or too high, leaving choice B and C. C is probably too high, as 5.55 is an approximation and so choice B is looking correct.

Do the calculations to confirm.
8.5 X 40/100 = 3.40 + 1.30 = $4.70.

6. A
First estimate the answer quickly in your head. One train is travelling at 72 km. and the other at 52 km. In one hour they will be 20 km. apart, so in 20 minutes they will be 20/3 = about 6.5 km.

Looking at the options, choices B and C are far to big and can be eliminated. Choice D is closer, but still too large, and can also be eliminated.

Do the calculations to confirm.
Distance traveled by 1st train in 20 minute = (72 km/hr×20 minutes)/60 minutes = 24 km
Distance traveled by 2nd train in 20 minute = (52 km/hr×20 minutes)/60 minutes = 17.33 km
Difference in distance = 24 - 17.33 = 6.67 km

7. C
Make a rough estimate in your head. Use 10% instead of 7%, so 425 + 10% = 467. Ignore the 1.6% for now and remember this is an estimate on the high side.

Choice A is too small and can be eliminated and choice D is too high and can be eliminated. That leaves choices B and C.

Do the calculations to confirm.
Let the original price be x, then at rate of 7% the discounted price will be = 0.93x
2% discounted amount then will be = 0.02 × 0.93x = 0.0186x
Remaining price = 0.93x - 0.0186x = 0.9114x
This is the amount which John has paid so
0.9114x = 425
x = 425/ 0.9114
x = $466.31

8. B

This question can be estimated in your head with a few shortcuts. 15% is difficult to work with so use 10% and 5%.
10% of 545 = 54.5
5% of 545 = about 27 (half of 10%)
Add them quickly in your head by estimating again.
Take 50 + 25 = 75 and add 7 for a rough approximation of 82. The actual number is 81.5.
Add 82 to 545. Again round to easy numbers to work with. take 550 + 82 = 632. Remember this is a high estimate. (The actual figure is 626.5)

Looking at the options, the only choice over 600 is Choice B.

Confirm by doing the calculations.
Actual cost = X, therefore, X = 545 + (545 X 0.15)
X = 545 + 81.75
X = 626.75

9. C

Estimate the answer first. The car is travelling at 60 km. and the motorbike is travelling at 40 km., which is 2/3 (40/60 = 2/3, or 2:3). So the motorcycle will take one-third longer to travel the same distance. If the car took 3.5 hours, the motorbike will take 3.5 + (1/3 of 3.5). 1/3 of 3.5 is going to be about 1.1, or say 1. 3.5 + 1 = 4.5.

Looking at the options, choice D can be eliminated right away. Choice A can be eliminated since it equals our estimate.

Do the calculations to confirm.
The distance covered by the car = 60 X 3.5 = 210 km.
Time required by the motorbike = 210/40 = 5.25 hr.

10. A

Do a quick estimate in your head and see if any options can be eliminated. Jim is travelling for 48 minutes at 40 km. per hour. If he was travelling for one hour, he would cover 40 km. Right away choice D can be eliminated because he is only travelling for a portion of an hour. Choice C, 38 km. is a very unlikely choice because it is so close to 40 and can be eliminated. The answer will be choice A or B.

Do the calculations to confirm.
Time to reach the office = 48 minutes. So if he covers 40 km in 60 minutes, then in 48 minutes, he will cover 48 X 40/60 = 32 km.

Essay Writing

Writing an essay can be a difficult process, especially if you have time constraints such as during an exam. Here are three simple steps to help you to write a solid, well thought out essay:

Essay Prompt: "In many communities, people volunteer to help others. Why is volunteering valuable, and how does it benefit both volunteers and those they help?"

Introduction

Volunteering—whether organizing a food drive, tutoring younger students, or cleaning up a neighborhood park—offers far more than just immediate assistance to those in need. Not only does it build stronger communities, but it also fosters empathy, leadership, and personal growth in volunteers. Because of these multifaceted benefits, volunteering remains a cornerstone of civic engagement today.

Commentary:

Hook: Begins with vivid examples to grab attention.

Context: Defines "volunteering" broadly and ties it to community impact.

Thesis (last sentence): Clearly states two main benefits—community strength and personal growth.

Body Paragraph 1

Topic sentence: First, volunteering enhances community cohesion and addresses pressing local needs.

Concrete evidence: When students in Riverdale organized a weekend food drive, they collected over 2,000 pounds of food, directly aiding local families facing food insecurity.

Commentary: This example shows how tangible results emerge from student efforts, which supports the thesis that communities benefit.

Concrete evidence: In another instance, neighbors working together to clean and plant trees in Elm Park reduced litter by 40% and increased park usage by 25%. Commentary: This further demonstrates that volunteering can transform shared spaces, directly linking to the idea of building a stronger community.

Closing sentence: Therefore, by bringing people together to solve local problems, volunteering strengthens connections and yields lasting improvements.

Commentary:

Structure: Follows the Schaffer method with CD–CM chunks
(details followed by twice as much commentary)

Transitions: Uses "therefore" to reinforce logical flow.

Body Paragraph 2
Topic sentence: Volunteering also brings unexpected personal rewards, cultivating empathy, leadership, and self-confidence.

Concrete evidence: A study from Stanford University found that high school volunteers reported a 30% increase in self-esteem and stronger leadership skills compared to their non-volunteering peers.

Commentary: This demonstrates quantifiable personal growth, validating the claim about volunteer benefits.

Concrete evidence: Anecdotally, Sarah Li, a teen tutor, said, "Explaining complex math problems helped me realize my own strengths and made me more patient."

Commentary: This personal insight enriches the argument—showing that volunteers grow not just in skill, but in character.

Closing sentence: In sum, by taking on volunteer roles, individuals not only give back but also build their own strengths and capacities.

Commentary:

Blends quantitative (study) and qualitative (personal anecdote) evidence.

Explicit commentary ensures each detail ties back to personal growth thesis.

Conclusion
Volunteering is more than a kind act—it is a powerful tool for social improvement and personal transformation. By joining forces to address community challenges, volunteers build stronger, more resilient neighborhoods. Similarly, by stepping into service roles, they gain empathy, confidence, and leadership skills. In a world increasingly marked by distance, volunteering reminds us that both societies and individuals thrive when we give our time and hearts. Ultimately, the true legacy of volunteering lies not just in what we do for others, but in how it reshapes us in the process.

Commentary:

Echoes key ideas from the introduction (community and personal growth).

Broader significance: Shows why volunteering matters "in a world increasingly marked by distance."

Graceful close—the final sentence reflects and expands on the thesis, giving the essay a sense of completion.

THE ESSAY WRITING PROCESS

Planning & Pre-writing

Brainstormed ideas: community service events, personal testimonials, research studies.

Chose clear thesis with two focused points—community and individual benefits.

Outlined body paragraphs with specific details paired with commentary (using the Schaffer structure: CD + 2×CM) .

Drafting the Introduction

Started with engaging examples to hook interest.

Provided context before landing on a tightly worded thesis.

Ensured thesis addresses the prompt directly.

Building Body Paragraphs

Used topic sentences that link each paragraph back to the thesis.

Each paragraph follows this mini-structure:

Topic sentence → 2. Detail → 3. Commentary → 4. (Repeat detail + commentary) → 5. Closing → transition.

Balanced factual (food drive stats, park usage, Stanford study) with personal (Sarah Li's quote) to add richness.

Writing Commentary

At least two commentary sentences per detail, weaving in analysis, interpretation, and personal reaction

Commentary explains why the detail matters, linking back to larger argument.

Crafting the Conclusion

Mirrored introduction's themes in reverse order for unity.

Went beyond summary to reflect on global relevance and lasting impact.

Avoided simply restating thesis; instead, offered insight on transformation.

Revision and Style

Removed first-person pronouns and contractions, kept formal tone.

Checked transitions and flow.

Proofread for grammar, clarity, and essay conventions.

Why This Essay Works
Structure: It follows a proven "five-paragraph" model—introduction, two detailed body paragraphs, and a conclusion—ideal for standardized tests.

Thesis: Precise and responsive to the prompt.

Evidence-Commentary Ratio: For every concrete fact, there are multiple sentences of analysis—ensuring depth.

Balance: Uses both statistical and human-level evidence.

Transitions and Cohesion: Logic connects each part smoothly.

Final Impact: Conveys broader significance and leaves a thoughtful closing impression.

Final Takeaways

Plan before writing—choose a thesis and gather supporting evidence.

Use the CD–CM model: a detail (quote, fact) followed by 2–3 sentences of commentary analyzing its relevance.

Craft clear topic sentences tying back to thesis.

Link sections with transitions ("Therefore," "In sum," "By stepping into...").

Conclude thoughtfully: echo your intro, and extend your insight.

Polish rigorously—check structure, avoid slang and contractions, proofread carefully.

Example Essay Prompts

Should high schools should require financial literacy courses before graduation? Support your position with specific reasons."

Think of a time when you faced a significant setback or failure. Describe how you responded, what you learned, and how it shaped you.

Describe a historical or literary figure you would like to interview. What questions would you ask, and why?

Some argue that participation in sports distracts from academics. Others believe athletics enrich student life. Take a position and defend your viewpoint.

COMMON ESSAY MISTAKES

Questioning authority makes society stronger. In every aspect our society, there is an authoritative person or group making rules. There is also the group underneath them who are meant to follow. 1 This is true of our country's public schools as well as our federal government. The right to question authority at both levels is guaranteed by the United States Declaration of Independence. People are given the ability to question so that authority figures are kept in check 2 and will be forced to listen to the opinions of other people. Questioning authority leads to positive changes in society and preserves what is already working well.

If students never question the authority of a principal's decisions, the best interest of the student body is lost. Good things 3 may not remain in place for the students and no amendment to the rules are sought. Change requires that authority be questioned. An example is Silver Head Middle School in Davie, Florida. Last year, the principal felt strongly about enforcing the school's uniform policy. Some students were not bothered by this. 4 Many students felt the policy disregarded their civil rights. A petition voicing student dissatisfaction was signed and presented to the principal. He met with a student representative to discuss the petition. Compromise was reached as a monthly "casual day." The students were able to promote change and peace by questioning authority.

Even at the level of federal government, our country's ultimate authority, the ability to question is the key to the harmony keeping society strong. Most government officials are elected by the public so they have the right to question their authority. 5 If there's a mandate, law, or statement that citizens aren't 6 happy with, they have recourse. Campaigning for, or against a political platform and participating in the electoral process give a voice to every opinion. I think elections are very important. 7 Without this questioning and examination of society's laws, the government will represent only the voice of the authority figure. The success of our society is based on the questioning of authority. 8

Society is strengthened by those who question authority. Dialogue is created between people with different visions and change becomes possible. At both the level of public school and of federal government, the positive effects of questioning authority can be witnessed. Whether questioning the decisions of a single principal or the motives of the federal government, it is the willingness of people to question and create change that allows society to grow. A strong society is inspired by many voices, all at different levels. 9 These voices keep society strong.

1. Write concisely. Combine the sentences to improve understanding and cut unnecessary words. Try: "In every aspect of society, there is an authority making rules and a group of people meant to follow them."

2. Avoid slang. Re-word "kept in check." Try: "People are given the ability to question so that authority figures are held accountable and will be forced to listen to the opinions of other people.

2-2. Cut unnecessary words. Try: "People are given the ability to question so that authority figures are held accountable and will listen to other opinions."

3. Use precise language. What are "good things?" Try: "Interesting activities may not remain in place for the students and no amendment to the rules are sought."

Use correct subject-verb agreement. Be careful to identify the correct subject of your sentence. Try: "Interesting activities may not remain in place for the students and no amendment to the rules is sought."

4. Don't add information that doesn't add value to your argument. Cut: "Some students weren't bothered by this."

5. Check for parallel structure. Who has the right to question whose authority? Try: "Having voted them in, the people have the authority to question public officials."

6. Don't use contractions in academic essays. Try: "If there is a mandate, law, or statement that citizens are not happy with, they have recourse."

7. Don't use the pronoun "I" in persuasive essays. Cut opinions. Cut: "I think elections are very important."

8. Use specific examples to prove your argument. Try: Discuss a particular election in depth.

9. Cut redundant sentences. Cut: "A strong society is inspired by many voices, all at different levels."

Writing Concisely

Concise writing is direct and descriptive. The reader follows the writer's thoughts easily. If your writing is concise, a four paragraph essay is acceptable for standardized tests. It's better to write clearly about fewer ideas than to write poorly about many.

This doesn't always mean using fewer words. It means that every word you use is important to the message. Unnecessary or repetitive information dilutes ideas and weakens your writing. The meaning of the word concise comes from the Latin, "to cut up." If it isn't necessary information, don't waste precious testing minutes writing it down.

Being redundant is a quick way to lengthen a sentence or paragraph, but it takes away your power during a timed essay. While many writers use repetition of phrases and key words to make their point, it's important to remove words that don't add value. Redundancy can confuse and lead you away from your subject when you need to write quickly. Be aware that many redundant phrases are part of our daily language and need to be cut from your essay.

For example, "bouquet of flowers" is a redundant phrase as only the word "bouquet" is necessary. Its definition includes flowers. Be especially careful with words you use to stress a point, such as "completely," "totally," and "very."

First of all, I'd like to thank my family.
Revised: First, I'd like to thank my family.

The school *introduced a new* rule.
Revised: The school introduced a rule.

I am *completely full.*
Revised: I am full.

Your glass is *totally empty*!
Revised: Your glass is empty!

Her artwork is *very unique.*
Revised: Her artwork is unique.

Other ways to cut bulk and time include avoiding phrases that have no meaning or power in your essay. Phrases like "in my opinion," "as a matter of fact," and "due to the fact that" are space and time wasters. Also, change passive verbs to active voice.

In my opinion, the paper is well written.
Revised: The paper is well written.

The book *was written* by the best students.
Revised: The best students wrote the book.

The teacher *is listening* to the students.
The teacher listens to the students.

This assigns action to the subject, shortens, and clarifies the sentence. When time is working against you, precise language is on your side.

Not only should you remove redundant phrases, whole sentences without value should be cut too. Replacing general nouns with specific ones is an effective way to accomplish this.

She screamed as the thing came closer. It was a sharp-toothed dog.

Revised: She screamed as the sharp-toothed dog came closer.

The revised sentence is precise and the paragraph is improved by combining sentences and varying sentence structure. When editing, ask yourself which thoughts should be connected and which need to be separated. Skim each paragraph as you finish writing it and cut as you go.

Leave three to four minutes for final editing. While reading, make a point to pause at every period. This allows you to "hear" sentences the way your reader will, not how you meant them to sound. This will help you find the phrases and sentences that need to be cut or combined. The result is an essay a grader will appreciate.

Avoiding Redundancy

Duplication and verbosity in English is the use of two or more words that clearly mean the same thing, making one of them unnecessary. It is easy to do use redundant expressions or phrases in a conversation where speech is spontaneous, and common in spoken English. In written English, however, redundancy is more serious and harder to ignore. Here are list of redundant phrases to avoid.

1. Suddenly exploded.

An explosion is instantaneous or immediate and that is sudden enough. No need to use 'suddenly' along with exploded.

2. Final outcome.

An outcome refers to the result. An outcome is intrinsically final and so no need to use final along with outcome.

3. Advance notice/planning/reservations/ warning.

A warning, notice, reservation or plan is made before an event. Once the reader sees any of these words, they know that they were done or carried out before the event. These words do not need to be used with advance.

4. First began, new beginning.

Beginning signals the start or the first time, and therefore the use of "new" is superfluous.

5. Add an additional.

The word 'add' indicates the provision of another something, and so "additional" is superfluous.

6. For a period/number of days.

The word "days" is already in plural and clearly signifies more than just one day. It is thus redundant to use "a number of," or "a period of" along with days. Simply state the number of days or of the specific number of days is unknown, you say 'many days.'

7. Foreign imports.

Imports are foreign as they come from another country, so it is superfluous to refer to imports as "foreign."

8. Forever and ever.

Forever indicates eternity and so there is no need for "ever" as it simply duplicated forever.

9. Came at a time when.

"At a time" is not necessary in this phrase because the 'when' already provides a temporal reference to the action, coming.

10. Free gift.

It cannot be a gift if it is paid for. A gift, by nature, is free and so referring to a gift is free is redundant.

11. Collaborate/join/meet/merge together.

The words merge, join, meet and collaborate already suggest people or things coming together. It is unnecessary to use any of these words with together, such as saying merge together or join together. The correct expression is to say, join or merge, omitting the together.

12. Invited guests.

Guests are those invited for an event. Since they had to be invited to be guests, there is no need to use invited with guests.

13. Major breakthrough.

A breakthrough is significant by nature. It can only be described as a breakthrough when there is a notable progress. The significant nature of the progress is already implied when you use the word "breakthrough," so "major" is redundant.

14. Absolutely certain or sure/essential/ guaranteed.

When someone or something is said to be sure or certain it indicates that it is without doubt. Using "absolutely" in addition to certain, or sure, is unnecessary. Essential or guaranteed is used for something that is absolute and so also does not need the word absolutely to accompany them.

15. Ask a question.

Ask means to present a question. Using “question” in addition to “ask” is redundant.

16. Basic fundamentals/essentials.

Using basic here is redundant. Essentials and fundamental suggest an elementary nature.

17. [Number] a.m. in the morning/p.m. in the evening.

When you write 8 a.m. the reader knows you mean 8 o’clock in the morning. It is not necessary to say 8 a.m. in the morning. Simply write 8 a.m. or 8 p.m.

18. Definite decision.

A decision is already definite even if it can be reversed later. A decision is a definite course of action has been chosen. No need to use the word definite along with the word decision.

19. Past history/record.

A record or history by definition refers to past events or occurrences. Using past to qualify history or record is unnecessary.

20. Consensus of opinion.

Consensus means agreement over something that may be or not be an opinion. So it may look that using the phrase ‘consensus of opinion’ is appropriate, but it is better to omit “opinion.”

How to Take a Test

https://www.test-preparation.ca/test-video/

EVERYONE KNOWS THAT TAKING AN EXAM IS STRESSFUL, BUT IT DOES NOT HAVE TO BE THAT BAD! There are a few simple things that you can do to increase your score on any type of test. Take a look at these tips and consider how you can incorporate them into your study time.

Reading the Instructions

This is the most basic point, but one that, surprisingly, many students ignore and it can cost them big time! Since reading the instructions is one of the most common, and 100% preventable mistakes, we have a whole section just on reading instructions.

Pay close attention to the sample questions. Almost all standardized tests offer sample questions, paired with their correct solutions. Go through these to make sure that you understand what they mean and how they arrived at the correct answer. Do not be afraid to ask the test supervisor for help with a sample that confuses you, or instructions that you are unsure of.

Tips for Reading the Question

We could write pages and pages of tips just on reading the test questions. Here are the ones that will help you the most.

- **Think first.** Before you look at the answer, read and think about the question. It is best to try to come up with the correct answer before you look at the options given. This way, when the test-writer tries to trick you with a close answer, you will not fall for it.

- **Make it true or false.** If a question confuses you, then look at each answer option and think of it as a "true" "false" question. Select the one that seems most likely to be "true."

- **Mark the Question.** Don't be afraid to mark up the test booklet. Unless you are specifically told not to mark in the booklet, use it to your advantage. More on this below.

- **Circle Key Words.** As you are reading the question, underline or circle key words. This helps you to focus on the most critical information needed to solve the problem. For example, if the question said, "Which of these is not a synonym for huge?" You might circle "not," "synonym" and "huge." That clears away the clutter and lets you focus on what is important.

- **Always underline these words:** all, none, always, never, most, best, true, false and except.

- **Cross out irrelevant choices.** If you find yourself confused by lengthy questions, cross out anything that you think is irrelevant, obviously wrong, or information that you think is offered to distract you. Elimination is the most valuable strategy!

- **Do not try to read between the lines.** Usually, questions are written to be straightforward, with no deep, underlying meaning. The simple answer really is often the correct answer. Do not over-analyze!

How to Take a Test - The Basics

Some tests are designed to assess your ability to quickly grab the necessary information; this type of exam makes speed a priority. Others are more concerned with your depth of knowledge, and how accurate it is. When you receive a test, look it over to determine whether the test is for speed or accuracy. If the test is for speed, like many standardized tests, your strategy is clear; answer as many questions as quickly as possible.

Watch out, though! There are a few tests that are designed to determine how fully and accurately you can answer the questions. Guessing on this type of test is a big mistake, because the teacher expects any student with an average grade to be able to complete the test in the time given. Racing through the test and making guesses that prove to be incorrect will cost you big time!

Every little bit helps - Calculators

Some calculators are permitted - see the guidelines here http://www.tasctest.com/tasc-test-calculators-for-test-takers.html

A calculator can really help! make sure you understand the guidelines and permitted models.

Make time your friend.

Budget your time from the moment your pencil hits the page until you are finished with the exam, and stick to it! Virtually all standardized tests have a time limit for each section. The time permitted for each section will almost certainly be included in the instructions or printed at the top of the page. If for some reason it is not immediately visible, rather than wasting your time hunting for it you can use the points or percentage of the score as a proxy to make an educated guess of the time limit.

Use the allotted time for each section and then move onto the next section whether you have completed it or not. Stick with the instructions and you will be able to answer most the questions in each section.

With speed tests you may not be able to complete the entire test. Rest assured that you are not really expected to! The goal of this type of examination is to determine how quickly you can reach into your brain and access a particular piece of information, which is one way of determining how well you know it. If you know a test you are taking is a speed test, you will know the strategies to use for the best results.

Easy does it.

One smart way to tackle a test is to locate the easy questions and answer those first. This is a time-tested strategy that never fails. First, read the question and decide if you can answer it in less than a minute. If so, complete the question and go to the next one. If not, skip it for now and continue to the next question. By the time you have completed the first pass through this section of the exam, you will have answered a good number of questions. Not only does it boost your confidence, relieve anxiety and kick your memory up a notch, you will know exactly how many questions remain and can allot the rest of your time accordingly. Think of doing the easy questions first as a warm-up!

If you run out of time before you manage to tackle all the difficult questions, do not let it throw you. All that means is you have used your time in the most efficient way possible by answering as many questions correctly as you could. Missing a few points by not answering a question whose answer you do not know just means you spent that time answering one whose answer you did.

A word to the wise: Skipping questions for which you are drawing a complete blank is one thing, but we are not suggesting you skip every question you come across that you are not 100 % certain of. A good rule of thumb is to try to answer at least eight of every 10 questions the first time through.

Do not watch your watch

At best, taking an important exam is an uncomfortable situation. If you are like most people, you might be tempted to subconsciously distract yourself from the task at hand. One of the most common ways is by becoming obsessed with your watch or the wall clock. Do not watch your watch! Take it off and place it on the top corner of your desk, far enough away that you will not be tempted to look at it every two minutes. Better still, turn the watch face away from you. That way, every time you try to sneak a peek, you will be reminded to refocus your attention to the task at hand. Give yourself permission to check your watch or the wall clock after you complete each section. Focus on answering the questions, not on how many minutes have elapsed since you last looked at it.

Divide and conquer.

What should you do when you come across a question that is so complicated you may not even be certain what is being asked? As we have suggested, the first time through the section you are best off skipping the question. However, at some point, you will need to return to it and get it under control. The best way to handle questions that leave you feeling so anxious you can hardly think is by breaking them into manageable pieces. Solving smaller bits is always easier. For complicated questions, divide them into bite-sized pieces and solve these smaller sets separately. Once you understand what the reduced sections are really saying, it will be much easier to put them together and get a handle on the bigger question.

Reason your way through the toughest questions.

If you find that a question is so dense you can't figure out how to break it into smaller pieces, there are a few strategies that might help. First, read the question again and look for hints. Can you re-word the question in one or more different ways? This may give you clues. Look for words that can function as either verbs or nouns, and try to figure out from the sentence structure which it is here. Remember that many nouns in English have several different meanings. While some of those meanings might be related, sometimes they are completely distinct. If reading the sentence one way does not make sense, consider a different definition or meaning for a key word.

The truth is, it is not always necessary to understand a question to arrive at a correct answer! A trick that successful students understand is using Strategy 5, Elimination. Frequently, at least one answer is clearly wrong and can be crossed off the list of possible correct answers. Next, look at the remaining answers and eliminate any that are only partially true. You may still have to flat-out guess from time to time, but using the process of elimination will help you make your way to the correct answer more often than not - even when you don't know what the question means!

Do not leave early.

Use all the time allotted to you, even if you can't wait to get out of the testing room. Instead, once you have finished, spend the remaining time reviewing your answers. Go back to those questions that were most difficult for you and review your response. Another good way to use this time is to return to multiple-choice questions in which you filled in a bubble. Do a spot check, reviewing every fifth or sixth question to make sure your answer coincides with the bubble you filled in. This is a great way to catch yourself if you made a mistake, skipped a bubble and therefore put all your answers in the wrong bubbles!

Become a super sleuth and look for careless errors. Look for questions that have double negatives or other odd phrasing; they might be an attempt to throw you off. Careless errors on your part might be the result of skimming a question and missing a key word. Words such as "always", "never", "sometimes" , "rarely" and the like can give a strong indication of the answer the question is really seeking. Don't throw away points by being careless!

Just as you budgeted time at the beginning of the test to allow for easy and more difficult questions, be sure to budget sufficient time to review your answers. On essay questions and math questions where you are required to show your work, check your writing to make sure it is legible.

Math questions can be especially tricky. The best way to double check math questions is by figuring the answer using a different method, if possible.

Here is another terrific tip. It is likely that no matter how hard you try, you will have a handful of questions you just are not sure of. Keep them in mind as you read through the rest of the test. If you can't answer a question, looking back over the test to find a different question that addresses the same topic might give you clues.

We know that taking the test has been stressful and you can hardly wait to escape. Just Leaving before you double-check as much as possible can be a quick trip to disaster. Taking a few extra minutes can make the difference between getting a bad grade and a great one. Besides, there will be lots of time to relax and celebrate after the test is turned in.

In the Test Room – What you MUST do!

If you are like the rest of the world, there is almost nothing you would rather avoid than taking a test. Unfortunately, that is not an option if you want to pass. Rather than suffer, consider a few attitude adjustments that might turn the experience from a horrible one to...well, an interesting one! Take a look at these tips. Simply changing how you perceive the experience can change the experience itself.

Get in the mood.

After weeks of studying, the big day has finally arrived. The worst thing you can do to yourself is arrive at the test site feeling frustrated, worried, and anxious. Keep a check on your emotional state. If your emotions are shaky before a test it can determine how well you do on the test. It is extremely important that you pump yourself up, believe in yourself, and use that confidence to get in the mood!

Don't fight reality.

Oftentimes, students resent tests, and with good reason. After all, many people do not test well, and they know the grade they end with does not accurately reflect their true knowledge. It is easy to feel resentful because tests classify students and create categories that just don't seem fair. Face it: Students who are great at rote memorization and not that good at actually analyzing material often score higher than those who might be more creative thinkers and balk at simply memorizing cold, hard facts. It may not be fair, but there it is anyway. Conformity is an asset on tests, and creativity is often a liability. There is no point in wasting time or energy being upset about this reality. Your first step is to accept the reality and get used to it. You will get higher marks when you realize tests do count and that you must give them your best effort. Think about your future and the career that is easier to achieve if you have consistently earned high grades. Avoid negative energy and focus on anything that lifts your enthusiasm and increases your motivation.

Get there early enough to relax.

If you are wound up, tense, scared, anxious, or feeling rushed, it will cost you. Get to the exam room early and relax before you go in. This way, when the exam starts, you are comfortable and ready to apply yourself. Of course, you do not want to arrive so early that you are the only one there. That will not help you relax; it will only give you too much time to sit there, worry and get wound up all over again.

If you can, visit the room where you will be taking your exam a few days ahead of time. Having a visual image of the room can be surprisingly calming, because it takes away one of the big 'unknowns'. Not only that, but once you have visited, you know how to get there and will not be worried about getting lost. Furthermore, driving to the test site once lets you know how much time you need to allow for the trip. That means three potential stressors have been eliminated all at once.

Get it down on paper.

One advantage of arriving early is that it allows you time to recreate notes. If you spend a lot of time worrying about whether you will be able to remember information like names, dates, places, and mathematical formulas, there is a solution for that. Unless the exam you are taking allows you to use your books and notes, (and very few do) you will have to rely on memory. Arriving early gives to time to tap into your memory and jot down key pieces of information you know will be asked. Just make certain you are allowed to make notes once you are in the testing site; not all locations will permit it. Once you get your test, on a small piece of paper write down everything you are afraid you will forget.

Get comfortable in your chair.

Here is a clever technique that releases physical stress and helps you get comfortable, even relaxed in your body. You will tense and hold each of your muscles for just a few seconds. The trick is, you must tense them hard for the technique to work. You might want to practice this technique a few times at home; you do not want an unfamiliar technique to add to your stress just before a test, after all! Once you are at the test site, this exercise can always be done in the rest room or another quiet location.

Start with the muscles in your face then work down your body. Tense, squeeze and hold the muscles for a moment or two. Notice the feel of every muscle as you go down your body. Scowl to tense your forehead, pull in your chin to tense your neck. Squeeze your shoulders down to tense your back. Pull in your stomach all the way back to your ribs, make your lower back tight then stretch your fingers. Tense your leg muscles and calves then stretch your feet and your toes. You should be as stiff as a board throughout your entire body.

Now relax your muscles in reverse starting with your toes. Notice how all the muscles feel as you relax them one by one. Once you have released a muscle or set of muscles, allow them to remain relaxed as you proceed up your body. Focus on how you are feeling as all the tension leaves. Start breathing deeply when you get to your chest muscles. By the time you have found your chair, you will be so relaxed it will feel like bliss!

Fight distraction.

A lucky few are able to focus deeply when taking an important examination, but most people are easily distracted, probably because they would rather be anyplace else! There are several things you can do to protect yourself from distraction.

Stay away from windows. If you sit near a window you are adding an unnecessary distraction.

Choose a seat away from the aisle so you do not become distracted by people who leave early. People who leave the exam room early are often the ones who fail. Do not compare your time to theirs.

Of course, you love your friends; that's why they are your friends! In the test room, however, they should become complete strangers inside your mind. Forget they are there. The first step is to physically distance yourself from friends or classmates. That way, you will not be tempted to glance at them to see how they are doing, and there will be no chance of eye contact that could either distract you or even lead to an accusation of cheating. Furthermore, if they are feeling stressed because they did not spend the focused time studying that you did, their anxiety is less likely to permeate your hard-earned calm.

Of course, you will want to choose a seat where there is sufficient light. Nothing is worse than trying to take an important examination under flickering lights or dim bulbs.

Ask the instructor or exam proctor to close the door if there is a lot of noise outside. If the instructor or proctor is unable to do so, block out the noise as best you can. Do not let anything disturb you.

Make sure you have enough pencils, pens and whatever else you will need. Many entrance exams do not permit you to bring personal items such as candy bars into the testing room. If so, be sure to eat a nutritionally balanced breakfast. Eat protein, complex carbohydrates and a little fat to keep you feeling full and to supercharge your energy. Nothing is worse than a sudden drop in blood sugar during an exam.

Do not allow yourself to become distracted by being too cold or hot. Regardless of the weather outside, carry a sweater, scarf or jacket if the air conditioning at the test site is set too high, or the heat set too low. By the same token, dress in layers so that you are prepared for a range of temperatures.

Drinking a gallon of coffee or gulping a few energy drinks might seem like a great idea, but it is, in fact, a very bad one. Caffeine, pep pills or other artificial sources of energy are more likely to leave you feeling rushed and ragged. Your brain might be clicking along, all right, but chances are good it is not clicking along on the right track! Furthermore, drinking coffee or energy drinks will mean frequent trips to the rest room. This will cut into the time you should be spending answering questions and is a distraction in itself, since each time you need to leave the room you lose focus. Pep pills will only make it harder for you to think straight when solving complicated problems.

At the same time, if anxiety is your problem try to find ways around using tranquilizers during test-taking time. Even medically prescribed anti-anxiety medication can make you less alert and even decrease your motivation. Being motivated is what you need to get you through an exam. If your anxiety is so bad that it threatens to interfere with your ability to take an exam, speak to your doctor and ask for documentation. Many testing sites will allow non-distracting test rooms, extended testing time and other accommodations with a doctor's note that explains the situation is made available.

Keep Breathing.

It might not make a lot of sense, but when people become anxious, tense, or scared, their breathing becomes shallow and, sometimes stop breathing all together! Pay attention to your emotions, and when you are feeling worried, focus on your breathing. Take a moment to remind yourself to breathe deeply and regularly. Drawing in steady, deep breaths energizes the body. When you continue to breathe deeply you will notice you exhale all the tension.

If you feel you need to, try rehearsing breathing at home. With continued practice of this relaxation technique, you will begin to know the muscles that tense up under pressure. Call these your "signal muscles." These are the ones that will speak to you first, begging you to relax. Take the time to listen to those muscles and do as they ask. With just a little breathing practice, you will get into the habit of checking yourself regularly and when you realize you are tense, relaxation will become second nature.

Avoid Anxiety Before a Test

Manage your time effectively.

This is a key to your success! You need blocks of uninterrupted time to study all the pertinent material. Creating and maintaining a schedule will help keep you on track, and will remind family members and friends that you are not available. Under no circumstances should you change your blocks of study time to accommodate someone else, or cancel a study session to do something more fun. Do not interfere with your study time for any reason!

Eat healthy.

Instead of reaching for the chips and chocolate, fresh fruits and vegetables are not only yummy but offer nutritional benefits that help to relieve stress. Some foods accelerate stress instead of reducing it and should be avoided. Foods that add to higher anxiety include artificial sweeteners, candy and other sugary foods, carbonated sodas, chips, chocolate, eggs, fried foods, junk foods, processed foods, red meat, and other foods containing preservatives or heavy spices. Instead, eat a bowl of berries and some yogurt!

Have confidence in yourself!

Everyone experiences some anxiety when taking a test, but exhibiting a positive attitude banishes anxiety and fills you with the knowledge you really do know what you need to know. This is your opportunity to show how well prepared you are. Go for it!

Do not chitchat with friends.

Let your friends know ahead of time that it is not anything personal, but you are going to ignore them in the test room! You need to find a seat away from doors and windows, one that has good lighting, and get comfortable. If other students are worried their anxiety could be detrimental to you; of course, you do not have to tell your friends that. If you are afraid they will be offended, tell them you are protecting them from your anxiety!

Common Test-Taking Mistakes

Taking a test is not much fun at best. When you take a test and make a stupid mistake that negatively affects your grade, it is natural to be very upset, especially when it is something that could have been easily avoided. So what are some of the common mistakes that are made on tests?

Put your name on the test!.

How could you possibly forget to put your name on a test? You would be amazed at how often that happens. Very often, tests without names are thrown out immediately, resulting in a failing grade.

Marking the wrong multiple-choice answer.

It is important to work at a steady pace, but that does not mean bolting through the questions. Be sure the answer you are marking is the one you mean to. If the bubble you need to fill in or the answer you need to circle is 'C', do not allow yourself to get distracted and select 'B' instead.

Answering a question twice.

Some multiple-choice test questions have two very similar answers. If you are in too much of a hurry, you might select them both. Remember that only one answer is correct, so if you choose more than one, you have automatically failed that question.

Mishandling a difficult question.

We recommend skipping difficult questions and returning to them later, but beware! First, be certain that you do return to the question. Circling the entire passage or placing a large question mark beside it will help you spot it when you are reviewing your test. Secondly, if you are not careful to skip the question, you can mess yourself up badly. Imagine that a question is too difficult and you decide to save it for later. You read the next question, which you know the answer to, and you fill in that answer. You continue to the end of the test then return to the difficult question only to discover you didn't actually skip it! Instead, you inserted the answer to the following question in the spot reserved for the harder one, thus throwing off the remainder of your test!

Incorrectly Transferring an answer from scratch paper.

This can happen easily if you are trying to hurry! Double check any answer you have figured out on scratch paper, and make sure what you have written on the test itself is an exact match!

Thinking too much.

Generally, your first thought is your best thought. If you worry yourself into insecurity, your self-doubts can trick you into choosing an incorrect answer when your first impulse was the right one!

Conclusion

CONGRATULATIONS! You have made it this far because you have applied yourself diligently to practicing for the exam and no doubt improved your potential score considerably! Passing your up-coming exam is a huge step in a journey that might be challenging at times but will be many times more rewarding and fulfilling. That is why being prepared is so important.

Good Luck!

Register for Free Updates and More Practice Test Questions

Register your purchase at

https://www.test-preparation.ca/register/ for updates and free test tips and more practice test questions.

Online Resources

How to Prepare for a Test - The Ultimate Guide

https://www.test-preparation.ca/prepare-test/

Learning Styles - The Complete Guide

https://www.test-preparation.ca/learning-style/

Test Anxiety Secrets!

https://www.test-preparation.ca/test-anxiety/

Time Management on a Test

https://www.test-preparation.ca/time-management/

Flash Cards - The Complete Guide

https://www.test-preparation.ca/flash-cards/

Test Preparation Video Series

https://www.test-preparation.ca/test-video/

How to Memorize - The Complete Guide

https://www.test-preparation.ca/memorize/

www.ingramcontent.com/pod-product-compliance
Lightning Source LLC
Chambersburg PA
CBHW072157090426
42740CB00012B/2305
* 9 7 8 1 9 2 8 0 7 7 2 6 8 *